What All Good Dogs Should Know

To our teachers:
all the dogs who have taught us how to train

What All Good Dogs Should Know

The Sensible Way to Train

Second Edition

Jack Volhard and Melissa Bartlett

WILEY

Wiley Publishing, Inc.

Howell Book House

Published by Wiley Publishing, Inc., Hoboken, New Jersey

For general information on our other products and services or to obtain technical support please contact our Customer Care Department within the U.S. at (800) 762-2974, outside the U.S. at (317) 572-3993, or fax (317) 572-4002.

Wiley also publishes its books in a variety of electronic formats. Some content that appears in print may not be available in electronic books. For more information about Wiley products, please visit our Web site at www.wiley.com.

Library of Congress Cataloging-in-Publication Data:
Volhard, Joachim.
What all good dogs should know : the sensible way to train /
Jack Volhard and Melissa Bartlett. —2nd ed.
    p. cm.
Includes bibliographical references.
ISBN 978-1-63026-253-2
1. Dogs—Training. 2. Dogs—Behavior. I. Bartlett, Melissa. II. Title.
SF431.V65 2008
636.7'0887—dc22

                        2007028199
        CIP

10   9   8   7   6   5   4   3

Second Edition

Book design by Erin Zeltner
Cover design by José Almaguer
Book production by Wiley Publishing, Inc. Composition Services

Contents

About the Authors

Jack Volhard, internationally known as a "trainer of trainers," is the recipient of six awards from the Dog Writers Association of America (DWAA). He is senior author of *Training Your Dog: The Step-by-Step Manual* (Howell Book House, 1983), named Best Care and Training Book for 1983 by the DWAA; *The Canine Good Citizen: Every Dog Can Be One* (Howell Book House, 1994), named Best Care and Training Book for 1994 by the DWAA; *Puppy Aptitude Testing*, named Best Film on Dogs in 1981; and, among other books, *Dog Training For Dummies* (Wiley Publishing, 2005). His books have been translated into four languages. He has also written numerous articles for various dog publications, and together with his wife, Wendy, produced four training videos.

For forty years he has taught obedience classes and given lectures, weekend seminars, and five-day training camps, teaching dog owners how to communicate with their pets and how to make training fun for both owners and their dogs, thereby achieving a mutually rewarding relationship.

Jack was an American Kennel Club Obedience Trial Judge for thirty-three years and is now an Obedience Judge Emeritus. He is also a member of the Hall of Fame of the International Association of Canine Professionals.

Melissa Bartlett's animal artwork has won top prizes nationally and has been featured in magazines such as *Sporting Classics* and *Just Labs*. She has also been named Dog Cartoonist of the Year by the Dog Writers Association of America, and her first article, "A Novice Looks at Puppy Aptitude Testing," published by the *AKC Gazette*, appeared in 1979. Since then her numerous articles and delightful illustrations have been included in various publications. In addition to co-authoring *What All Good Dogs Should Know*, she has illustrated three other books on dog training.

Years ago, she trained her first obedience dog with Jack and Wendy Volhard. Since then she has gone on to successfully compete with her own dogs in conformation, obedience, and carting events, as well as instruct dog-training classes for the family pet. Melissa and her Bernese Mountain Dog are a familiar sight at local schools, nursing homes, and retirement centers doing dog-therapy work. She is also an active advocate for shelter dogs and rescue groups and owns a rescued Australian Shepherd.

Chapter 1

Why Train Your Dog and When to Start

Trained dogs are "free" dogs. They are welcome almost anywhere because they behave themselves around people and other dogs, they stay when told, and they come when called. They are a pleasure to take for a walk and can be let loose for a romp in the park. They can be taken on trips and family outings. They are members of the family in every sense of the word.

A trained dog spends more time with his family than an untrained dog.

1

On the other hand, untrained dogs have few, if any, privileges. When guests come, they are locked away because they are too unruly. When the family sits down to eat, they are locked up or put outside because of begging at the table. They are never allowed off leash because they don't come when called. Nobody wants to take them for a walk because they pull, and family outings with such a nuisance are unimaginable.

Your dog—for simplicity, we call him Felix throughout this book—has a life expectancy of 8 to 16 years. Now is the time to ensure that these years are going to be mutually rewarding. For your sanity and his safety, train your dog. Teach him what every *good* dog should know.

WHAT IS A GOOD DOG?

Many dog books tell you that dogs are loyal, obedient, trustworthy, good with children, born protectors, and wonderful companions. Most dogs have the potential to

The perfect pet.

be great pets, but few are born that way. Almost all require some training to bring out the best in them.

A good dog should:

- Be housetrained.
- Come when called.
- Have no bad habits.
- Stay when told.
- Not pull when taken for a walk.

Depending on your dog and what you expect from him, he may need training in just a few of these areas or in all five.

WHAT IS INVOLVED IN TRAINING?

It may come as a surprise to you, but your dog's ancestors were bred for their ability to do a particular job well. Looks were considered coincidental. How readily you can train your dog to fit into your lifestyle depends on the job for which he was bred. For example, a dog bred for guarding is easier to train to stay on the property than a dog bred for hunting.

Today, most owners—and we suspect you did, too—choose their pets on the basis of appearance—"What a cute puppy!" But when you selected your dog, did you consider how the instincts for which he was selectively bred over the course of countless generations would affect his behavior as an adult?

Fortunately, some of these instincts are the very ones that endear the dog to you and make him such a good pet—the legendary protectiveness of children, the warning bark when a stranger comes on the property, the friendly greeting when you come home, and the comfort he provides in times of sorrow. Characteristics of specific breeds, such as the Newfoundland's rescue instincts, the Bernese Mountain Dog's willingness to pull a cart, the terrier's untiring playfulness, and the Labrador's eagerness to retrieve for his master, are equally appealing.

However, other instinctive behaviors get the dog into trouble. A dog bred for guarding who does his job *too* well may be accused of being vicious; one bred for herding may be chastised for chasing children, joggers, bicycles, and cars; and the hunting dog may be reprimanded for pulling on the leash when following a scent. Only the lap dog can get away with almost anything.

> If what you are trying to teach your dog is in harmony with his instincts, training him will be easy; if it goes against the dog's instincts, your task will be more difficult. For example, it will be easier to teach a Labrador to retrieve than to teach a herding dog not to chase joggers.

Remember that a cute puppy can be a handful as an adult.

For Barbara and Ed, it was love at first sight with Bentley, a Mastiff puppy. On impulse, they brought Bentley home from the pet store. When he grew into a huge dog and took to knocking down the mailman, Barbara and Ed were horrified. "He was such a cuddly puppy," they recalled, "just like a teddy bear." They did not realize that Bentley was just doing his job—Mastiffs were bred in England to guard estates. With a little training, plus keeping an eye on Bentley when the mailman was expected, the problem was resolved.

Newfoundlands were bred for rescue.

Sometimes instincts get a dog into trouble.

WHEN TO BEGIN TRAINING

Whether your dog is a puppy, an adolescent, or an adult dog, start training him now. There is no truth in the saying "Old dogs can't learn new tricks"—it just takes longer. For a puppy, the ideal time to begin training is at 7 weeks of age. Your puppy is most receptive to training during an 8-week window from 7 to 16 weeks. You will be amazed at the ease and speed with which a puppy learns. The longer you wait, the harder the job will become. Make the most of the available time now!

During this period your puppy is capable of learning far more than you will teach him. What the puppy learns now he will remember for the rest of his life. His brain is the same size as that of an adult dog; he lacks only the experience and motor coordination of an adult dog.

We know what you're thinking: "I have plenty of time. I can wait until he's 6 months to a year old. Let him enjoy his puppyhood." While you may have the best of intentions, your thinking is flawed. Why? There are three reasons:

1. Your puppy *is* going to learn many things while he is growing up, with or without your involvement. Some of the behaviors he will probably learn are the very ones you don't want him to do as an adult dog; for example, dashing outside, pulling on the leash, not coming when called, and jumping on people. The more ingrained these behaviors become, the greater the difficulty in eliminating them.

2. Learning at this stage is perhaps even more important than any specific commands you want to teach Felix. Future lessons you want your dog to learn are easier to teach to a dog who had some training as a puppy. Besides, puppies like to learn, and your puppy will look forward to his training sessions.

Begin training as soon as you get your dog.

3. Puppies are physically easier to manipulate than grown dogs. Again, you don't have much time—at 7 months of age dogs reach about 70 percent of their full size.

Developmental periods

As your puppy grows up, he will go through various developmental periods. These periods, in turn, influence how he responds to training.

The first major period that influences training occurs sometime between the fourth and eighth months, when your puppy realizes there is a big, wide world out there. Up to now, chances are the puppy followed your every footstep and perhaps even willingly came to you every time you called him. But now he wants to do his own thing—investigate a scent, follow a trail, chase a butterfly, whatever. He is maturing and cutting the apron strings. This is normal behavior. Your puppy is not being spiteful or disobedient, he's just becoming an adolescent.

While Felix is going through this phase, it is best to keep him on leash or in a confined area until you have *taught* him to come when called. Otherwise, not coming when called will become an annoying and potentially dangerous habit. Once it becomes an established behavior, it will be difficult to change, so prevention is the best cure. Chapter 9 explains how to teach your dog to come when called.

Puppies develop into adolescents between 4 and 8 months of age.

Under *no* circumstances should you chase after your dog, as he will think you are playing his game. Instead, run the other way and try to get him to chase *you*. If that does not work, kneel down and pretend you have found something extremely interesting on the ground, hoping your dog's curiosity will make him come to you. If you do have to go to your dog, approach *slowly* until you can calmly take him by the collar.

The need to socialize

Your dog is a social animal. To become an acceptable pet, he needs to interact with you, your family, and other humans, as well as dogs. If denied that chance, his behavior around other people or dogs may be unpredictable, either fearful or aggressive. For example, unless he regularly meets children during this period, he may not be trustworthy around them, especially when he feels cornered.

Your puppy needs the opportunity to meet and to have positive experiences with those people who will play a role in his life. If you are a grandparent whose grandchildren occasionally visit, have your puppy meet children as often as possible. If you live by yourself, make an effort to let your puppy meet other people, especially friends and members of the opposite sex. Interacting with other dogs on a regular basis as he is growing up is equally important.

If you plan to take Felix on family outings or vacations, get him used to riding in a car. Time spent on socializing *now* is worth the effort in making your puppy a well-adjusted companion. Puppyhood is short and goes by quickly, so use this time wisely.

Make sure to socialize your puppy.

BUILDING TRUST

Picture your dog getting loose and chasing a cat across the road. Your heart is in your mouth because you are afraid a car might hit him. When he finally returns, you are angry and soundly scold him for chasing the cat and giving you such a scare.

How your dog perceives coming to you.

Here is how your *dog* looks at this situation. First, he chased the cat, which was a lot of fun. Then he came back to you and was reprimanded, which was no fun at all. What you wanted to teach him was not to chase the cat. What you *actually* taught him was that coming to you is unpleasant.

One of the commands you will want to teach Felix is to come when called. To be successful, remember this principle: *Whenever your dog comes to you, be nice to him.* Reward this behavior. No matter what your dog might have done, be pleasant and greet him with a kind word, a pat on the head, and a smile. Teach your dog to trust you by being a safe place for him. When he is with you, follows you, or comes to you, make him feel wanted.

When you call your dog to you and then punish him, you undermine his trust in you. When your dog comes to you voluntarily and gets punished, he associates being punished with coming to you.

You might ask "How can I be nice to my dog when he brings me the remains of one of my brand new shoes, or when he wants to jump on me with muddy paws, or when I just discovered an unwanted present on the carpet?" For the answers, you will have to read this book; it will show you how to deal with all these situations without undermining his trust in you.

Always make your dog feel wanted when he comes to you.

CONSISTENCY IS KEY

If there is any magic to training, it is consistency. Your dog cannot understand *sometimes, maybe,* or *only on Sundays.* He *can* understand what is acceptable behavior and what is not.

For example, it is confusing for Felix if you permit him to jump on you when you are wearing old clothes, but then get angry with him when he joyfully plants muddy paws on your best suit.

Tom loved to wrestle with Tyson, his Boxer. Then one day, when Grandma came to visit, Tyson flattened her. Tom was angry, and Tyson was confused—he thought roughhousing was a wonderful way to show affection. After all, that's what Tom taught him.

> Training your dog is a question of who is more persistent—you or your dog. Some commands he will learn quickly, others will take more time. If several attempts don't bring success, be patient, remain calm, and try again. It sometimes takes many repetitions before a dog understands a command and responds to it each and every time.

Does this mean you can never permit your puppy to jump up on you? Not at all, but you have to train him that he may *only* do so when you tell him it's "OK." But beware: Training a dog to make this distinction is more difficult than training him not to jump up at all. The more "black and white" you can make it, the easier it is for your dog to understand what you want.

Don't encourage your dog to roughhouse.

TAKING CHARGE

Taking charge is not a matter of choice. Dogs are pack animals and you and your family are now his pack. As far as he is concerned, no pack can exist without a leader, and it's either you or him. That's the way it *has* to be.

Few dogs actively seek leadership and most are perfectly content, and actually prefer, for you to assume the role of pack leader. But you *must* do so, or even the meekest of dogs will take over. Remember, it's not a matter of choice. If you expect your dog to listen to you and obey your commands, he has to accept you as his pack leader.

If your dog takes over your favorite armchair, constantly demands attention, ignores you when you want him to move, or shoots outside ahead of you when you open the door, he is in charge instead of you. Part of his behavior may be due to a lack of education, so the first order of business is to begin training him. Start by teaching him to sit on command (see chapter 6) and to lie down on command (see chapter 7). Both of these exercises not only help you to control your dog, which is an important part of dog ownership, but they also teach your dog that you are in charge.

Even the meekest dog will take over if you don't assume the role of pack leader.

Dogs are calmer when their owner is in charge.

After you have trained your dog, use the commands you have taught him on a regular basis. For example, have him sit before doing any of the following:

- Giving him a treat
- Putting down his food bowl
- Petting him
- Letting him go through a door

Toshiba, Richard's Akita, constantly crashed through doors ahead of her owner, ignored commands, and growled when Richard wanted her off the sofa. Richard realized he had to train Toshiba. He trained her to sit and behave before she was petted or got any treats, and to stay off the furniture and lie on the rug instead. What most impressed Richard was the change in Toshiba's attitude: She seemed calmer, more relaxed, and happier. "I guess she really wanted me to be in charge all along," Richard commented.

WHERE TO TRAIN

When you begin your training, do it in an area familiar to your dog and one that is relatively free of distractions so that you are his center of attention. Such an area can be a room in your house where the two of you can be alone or your backyard. Avoiding distractions in the beginning will speed up the learning process.

After Felix has learned to respond to a particular command in this setting, take him to a new location without too many distractions, such as a quiet park or an empty parking lot, to practice. Finally, practice in the presence of distractions, such as other people and children.

Felix will not be fully reliable until you practice the commands you have taught him under conditions when you need him to respond. For example, to prevent Felix from jumping up on guests to your home, you need to teach him to sit and stay, and you need to practice by having a friend or neighbor come to the door, ring the bell, and have Felix sit and stay as you open the door. (See chapter 6 for more on the Sit and Stay commands.)

Facts from Felix

1)   A trained dog is a free dog.

2)   Start training your dog as soon as you get him.

3)   Whenever your dog comes to you, be nice to him.

4)   If there is any magic to training, it is consistency.

5)   As far as your dog is concerned, no pack can exist without a leader.

6)   For your sanity and his safety, you have to be the one in charge.

Chapter 2

A Personality Profile for Your Dog

Your dog was born with a set of instinctive behaviors that he inherited from his parents. These behaviors, which can be grouped into three broad categories—prey, pack, and defense—are collectively called *drives*. The number of behaviors a dog has in each drive determines his temperament, his personality, and how he perceives the world.

BEHAVIORS IN EACH DRIVE

A dog's *prey drive* includes those innate behaviors associated with hunting, killing prey, and eating. This drive is activated by motion, sound, and smell. Behaviors associated with the prey drive are seeing; hearing; scenting; tracking; stalking; chasing anything that moves; pouncing; high-pitched barking; jumping up; pulling down; shaking, tearing, and ripping apart; carrying; eating; digging; and burying.

You see these behaviors when your dog is chasing a cat or when he gets excited and barks in a high-pitched tone of voice as the cat climbs up a tree. Your dog may also shake and rip apart soft toys and bury dog biscuits in the couch.

The *pack drive* includes behaviors associated with social interaction with other dogs; playing; and reproductive behaviors such as licking, mounting, washing ears, and all courting gestures. In the case of a dog, the ability to be part of a group translates itself into a willingness to work with you as part of a team.

A dog who exhibits many of these behaviors is the one who follows you around the house, is happiest when he's with you, loves to be petted and groomed, and likes to work with you. Such a dog may be unhappy when left alone for long periods.

The three drives, or instinctive behaviors, of a dog.

Finally, the *defense drive* consists of the instincts for survival and self-preservation, and includes both fight and flight behaviors. The defense drive is more complex than prey and pack drives, because the same situation that can make some dogs aggressive (fight) can also elicit avoidance (flight) behaviors in others, especially in young dogs.

Fight behaviors tend not to fully develop until the dog is over 2 years of age, although tendencies toward these behaviors will be seen at an earlier age. Examples of fight behaviors are a dog who "stands tall," stares at other dogs, or likes to strut his stuff. He stands his ground with his ears and whiskers pointed forward and his tail held up. He goes toward unfamiliar objects or situations, and his hackles go up from his shoulders to his neck. He may guard his food, toys, or territory from other dogs or people, and he may dislike being petted or groomed. Such a dog refuses to move when lying in front of doorways or cupboards, making his owner walk around him.

Flight behaviors demonstrate that the dog is unsure about something. Examples are hackles that go up the full length of the body, not just at the neck; hiding or running away from new situations; a dislike of being touched by strangers; or a general lack of confidence. Young dogs tend to exhibit more flight behaviors than older dogs. *Freezing* (not going forward or backward) is generally considered inhibited flight behavior.

YOUR DOG'S PERSONALITY

To help you understand your dog's behaviors, Jack and Wendy Volhard cataloged ten behaviors exhibited in each drive and created the Canine Personality Profile (see below). The ten behaviors chosen are the most representative for each drive and are easily recognized by most dog owners.

 The results of the Profile will give you a good starting point for understanding why your dog does what he does. This understanding will help you make his training a positive and enjoyable experience for both of you.

When completing the following Profile, keep in mind that it was devised for a house dog with an enriched environment and not a dog tied out back or kept solely in a kennel; such dogs have fewer opportunities to express as many behaviors as a house dog. Your answers should indicate the behaviors your dog *would* exhibit if he had not already been trained to do otherwise. For example, did he jump up on the counter to steal food before he was trained not to do so?

When completing the Profile, assign the following point values to your answers:

Almost always—10

Sometimes—5

Hardly ever—0

If you have not had the chance to observe all of these behaviors, then leave the answer blank.

Canine Personality Profile

When presented with the opportunity, does your dog . . .

1. Sniff the ground or air? _____
2. Get along with other dogs? _____
3. Stand his ground or show curiosity toward strange objects or sounds? _____
4. Run away from new situations? _____
5. Get excited by moving objects, such as bikes or squirrels? _____
6. Get along with people? _____
7. Like to play tug-of-war games to win? _____
8. Hide behind you when he feels he can't cope? _____
9. Stalk cats, other dogs, or things in the grass? _____

10. Bark when he's left alone?   _____

11. Bark or growl in a deep tone of voice?   _____

12. Act fearfully in unfamiliar situations?   _____

13. Bark in a high-pitched voice when excited?   _____

14. Solicit petting, or like to snuggle with you?   _____

15. Guard his territory?   _____

16. Tremble or whine when unsure?   _____

17. Pounce on his toys?   _____

18. Like to be groomed?   _____

19. Guard his food or toys?   _____

20. Cower or lie on his back when reprimanded?   _____

21. Shake and "kill" his toys?   _____

22. Seek eye contact with you?   _____

23. Dislike being petted?   _____

24. Act reluctant to come close to you when called?   _____

25. Steal food or garbage?   _____

26. Follow you around like a shadow?   _____

27. Guard his owner(s)?   _____

28. Have difficulty standing still when groomed?   _____

29. Like to carry things in his mouth?   _____

30. Play a lot with other dogs?   _____

31. Dislike being groomed?   _____

32. Cower or cringe when a stranger bends over him?   _____

33. Wolf down his food?   _____

34. Jump up to greet people?   _____

35. Like to fight other dogs?   _____

36. Urinate during greeting behavior?   _____

37. Like to dig and/or bury things?   _____

38. Show reproductive behaviors, such as mounting other dogs?   _____

39. Get picked on by older dogs when he was a young dog?   _____

40. Tend to bite when cornered?   _____

Scoring the profile

Next to each number in the following table, enter the point value you have given that question, and then total each column in the space provided.

Prey	Pack	Fight	Flight
1.	2.	3.	4.
5.	6.	7.	8.
9.	10.	11.	12.
13.	14.	15.	16.
17.	18.	19.	20.
21.	22.	23.	24.
25.	26.	27.	28.
29.	30.	31.	32.
33.	34.	35.	36.
37.	38.	39.	40.
Total Prey:	Total Pack:	Total Fight:	Total Flight:

What the scores mean

Not surprisingly, the results of the Profile tend to be breed-specific:

- If your dog was bred to hunt or herd—think Labrador and Border Collie—he probably scored highest in prey drive, followed by pack, with fight somewhere below 50 points, and a few flight behaviors.

- If he was bred to guard or protect—think German Shepherd—his score for fight behaviors will likely be well above 50 points, with perhaps a few flight behaviors, but still many prey and pack behaviors.

- A dog bred for drafting—think Bernese Mountain Dog—should score high in pack, low in fight, and have few prey behaviors. (You would not want him to chase after a cat with his little cart bouncing behind.)

- If you have a "designer dog" (Pugle, Labradoodle, Schnoodle, etc.) or a mixed breed, his drive numbers will not be as predictable.

Most dogs are high in prey drive, which makes sense in light of the majority of the tasks they were bred to perform. Unfortunately, it is also the drive that is the most irritating to you, his owner, and the one that can get the dog into trouble. When you take him for a walk, chances are good that he pulls you here, there, and everywhere, with his nose on the ground following various scents. When he spots a squirrel, he sets off in hot pursuit and ignores your calls. When left in the yard, he digs holes and barks at passing cars.

A high prey drive often gets a dog into trouble.

NOW WHAT?

Before you can use the results of the Profile, first take a look at what you are trying to teach Felix (our name for your dog) and which drive he has to be in to respond to a given command.

Felix needs to be in pack drive for most of the commands you want him to know, such as walking on leash without pulling, being able to sit and stay, being able to go lie down, and being able to come when called. Responding to these commands requires him to be in pack drive, which means being with you or doing something for you. You certainly don't want him to be in prey (chase) or defense drive (guard or flee). All else being equal, a dog with many pack behaviors (more than 60 points) will have no difficulty learning these commands.

BRINGING OUT DRIVES

Here are the basic rules for bringing out specific drives in your dog:

- **Prey drive** is brought out in your dog by the use of motion: hand movements; using a high-pitched tone of voice or an object of attraction (defined as anything the dog will actively work for, such as a stick, toy, or food); chasing or being chased; and leaning backward with your body.
- **Pack drive** is brought out by physical affection, verbal praise, and smiling at your dog. Grooming and playing also bring out pack-drive behaviors.
- **Defense drive** is brought out by leaning over the dog, either from the front or the side; *checking* (a sharp tug on the leash); and using a harsh tone of voice.

Changing the dog's behavior from prey drive to pack drive.

As an example, let's take a look at a fairly common situation. You are trying to teach Felix to walk on a loose leash in the yard when a squirrel scampers up a nearby tree. Felix spots it and immediately gives chase, straining at the end of the leash and barking his head off. You call him and try to get his attention back on you, but he is totally focused on the squirrel. Felix is in full-blown prey drive.

What can you do to get his mind off the squirrel? Or, in technical terms, get him out of prey drive and into pack drive, where he is supposed to be? As you've already discovered, calling Felix does not work. You could try bribing him with a tasty treat or toy, but that would probably not do the trick. Even a nice piece of meat would probably not work. If you had a bigger squirrel—not a likely occurrence!—that might get his attention back on you.

The simplest way to get his attention back on you is a firm check on the leash, followed by praise when he looks at you and gives up on the squirrel. And you may have to do that several times before he will obey a voice command.

PRACTICAL APPLICATION

By looking at your dog's Profile, you will know what type of training will work best for him and where you need to concentrate your training efforts. Following are a few of the more common Profiles we see in our training classes:

- **Defense (fight)—more than 60 points.** Your dog will not be bothered too much by a firm hand. Body posture is not critical, although inconsistencies on your part will slow down the training. Tone of voice should be firm, but pleasant and nonthreatening.

With the high-defense (fight) dog, establish your leadership through training exercises.

- **Defense (flight)—30 or more points.** Correct body posture, gentle handling, and quiet, pleasant tone of voice are critical. Avoid using a harsh tone of voice and any hovering—leaning over or toward your dog.

- **Prey—more than 60 points.** Your dog will respond well to the use of treats or a toy during teaching. He may need a firm hand, depending on the strength of his defense drive (fight), to suppress the prey drive when in high gear, such as when chasing a cat or spotting a squirrel. He's easily motivated, but also easily distracted by motion or moving objects. Signals mean more to this dog than verbal commands. You will need to use your body, hands, and leash correctly so as not to confuse him.

- **Prey—less than 60 points.** Your dog is probably not easily motivated by food or other objects, but is also not easily distracted by moving objects.

- **Pack—more than 60 points.** Your dog likes to be with you and will respond with little guidance. He responds readily to praise and touch.

- **Pack—less than 40 points; prey—more than 50 points.** Your dog may not care whether he is with you or not. He likes to do his own thing, but if he has sufficient prey behaviors, he can be trained with the use of treats or toys. Often breed specific for dogs bred to work independently of humans, like Huskies and sight hounds.

Facts from Felix

1) Motion, sounds, and odors put your dog into prey drive.

2) Touching and a friendly voice put your dog into pack drive.

3) Physical discomfort and an unfriendly voice put your dog into defense drive.

4) A dog with many prey behaviors needs lots of training around distractions.

5) A dog with more pack behaviors than prey behaviors is easy to train.

6) Your dog's Profile tells you the correct way to train him.

Yes, dogs can think. The problem is, they think like dogs.

Chapter 3

How Your Dog Thinks

O f course, dogs think. They can also problem solve. Unlike people, however, they are unable to reason. And just like people, some are smarter than others. In this chapter, you'll explore how your dog thinks and how you can tell what he is thinking about.

CAN YOUR DOG READ YOUR MIND?

Dogs often give the appearance of being able to read your mind. What happens in actuality is that by observing you, and studying your habits and movements, they learn to anticipate your actions. Since dogs communicate with each other through body language, they quickly become experts at reading yours.

For example, before leaving for work, Marcia always put Bella in her crate. It wasn't long before Bella went into her crate on her own when Marcia was about to leave. "What a clever puppy," thought Marcia. "She knows I'm going to work."

What Bella observed was that just before leaving for work, Marcia put on her makeup and then crated her. Bella's cue to go into her crate was Marcia's putting on her makeup. Then one evening, before dinner guests were to arrive, Marcia started putting on makeup. When Bella immediately went into her crate, Marcia realized her dog had not been reading her mind, but had learned her routine through observation.

"READING" YOUR DOG

Just as your dog Felix takes his cues from watching *you*, so can you learn to interpret what he is thinking by watching *him*. The more time you spend observing your dog, the better you get at interpreting what's on his mind.

Interrupt, then give the command.

From prior observation, you know Felix has the habit of *counter surfing*—putting his front feet on the counter to see whether there is anything edible up there he can steal. Since he has done this a number of times before, you recognize his intentions by the look on his face—head and ears are up, whiskers pointed forward, intent stare—and the way he moves in the direction of the counter—deliberately, with his tail wagging in happy anticipation.

At that precise point you should *interrupt* Felix's thoughts. When he is *thinking* about something you don't want him to do is the ideal time to intervene.

In a stern voice say, "Not so fast young man," or "Stop," or "Ah, ah," or sharply clap your hands. Then give him a command incompatible with "counter surfing," such as "Sit" (see chapter 6) or "Down" (see chapter 7).

Second choice—catch him in the act.

If you catch Felix in the act of trying to steal food—he already has his front paws planted on the counter—firmly tell him to stop, take him by his collar, and physically remove his paws from the counter.

Oops—too late!

Visualize yourself preparing a piece of meat for dinner. You leave the counter to answer the phone and upon your return, the meat is gone. You know Felix ate it. Your first reaction is anger. Immediately Felix looks guilty, and you *assume* it is because he knows he has done wrong.

In fact, Felix knows no such thing. He is reacting to your anger and wonders why you are angry, and, perhaps based on prior experience, expects to be the target of your wrath.

Do not attempt any discipline *after* the offending deed has been accomplished. Your dog cannot make the connection between the discipline and what he just did. Your dog may look guilty, but not because he understands what he has done; he looks guilty only because he understands you are upset.

Unless you can catch him in the act, or, ideally, while he is thinking about stealing the meat, reprimands are too late. If he has the meat in his mouth, take it away from him. If he has already eaten the meat, it's too late to do anything on your part—the meat is gone, and you should do nothing after the *fait accompli*. (Moral of the story: Don't leave meat unattended on the counter!)

Communicating with your dog

We do not recommend using the word "no" in training your dog. Just yelling "No!" at the poor dog for everything and anything will only confuse him and make him neurotic. There is no exercise called "No." Instead, be specific when training your dog. Tell him what you *want* him to do rather than what you don't want him to do. If you don't want him to jump on you, for example, tell him to "Sit."

Similarly, avoid (get out of the habit of) using your dog's name as a reprimand or as a substitute for a command, because this just leaves the poor dog to try and figure out what you want. Use the name of your dog to get his attention and then follow with a command, such as "Felix, sit." When you call your dog's name, he should consider it a pleasant experience.

Communicate with your dog in a positive manner. Listen to yourself when you interact with your dog. Do you sound pleasant and positive, or unpleasant and negative?

Do not attempt any discipline after the fact.

Instead of telling your dog what you don't want him to do, train him to respond to specific commands so that you can tell him what you want him to do. Put him in a position where you can praise him and tell him how good he is.

> 🐾 The most difficult part of training a dog involves eliminating two bad habits: using the word "no" as a way to communicate and using his name as a reprimand or a substitute for a specific command. Focus on teaching your dog what you want him to do and ignore what you don't want him to do.

Your dog is a dog

Your efforts to train your dog are doomed to failure if you think he has human standards and reasoning abilities. He certainly does not experience guilt. Blaming the dog because "he ought to know better" or "he shouldn't have done it" or "how could he do this to me" will not improve his behavior. He also does not "understand every word you say"—if he did, he would not need training.

INTERPRETING YOUR DOG'S BODY POSTURES

The following six body postures will help you interpret what's on Felix's mind.

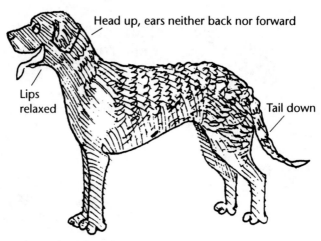

Relaxed: "I'm calm and ready to learn."

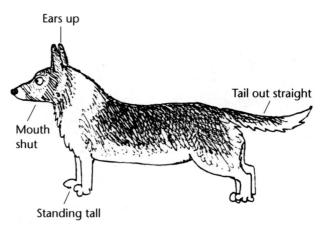

Alert: "What's going on?"

Relaxed

A relaxed dog is calm and ready to be trained. You can easily get his attention focused on you.

Alert

An alert dog has sensed something. It could be the family car approaching, a cat, another dog, or the mail carrier. What comes next depends on your dog's temperament. For example, if it is a cat, Felix may be thinking about giving chase. *Now* is the right time to tell him to forget about the cat. Remove him from the location or tell him to "Sit" and "Stay."

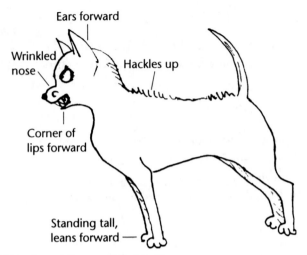

Ears forward

Wrinkled nose

Hackles up

Corner of lips forward

Standing tall, leans forward

Aggressive: "Watch out! I'm ready to bite!"

Aggressive

This position warns that the dog may bite. If this is not your dog, stay away from him. If it is your dog, you need help from a professional dog trainer.

Appeasing

This stance signals "I want to be friends." Felix is pleased to be in the presence of someone he considers superior. He is not feeling guilty, but is doing everything possible to let you know that he is going along with whatever you say. If this is a puppy, or a submissive adult, he may urinate. Do not discipline him for urinating because it will only make it worse. Avoid a harsh tone of voice, eye contact, and hovering over the dog. Just ignore him for a while.

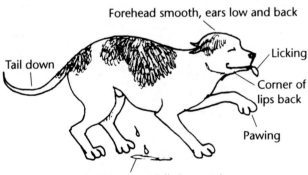

Forehead smooth, ears low and back

Tail down

Licking

Corner of lips back

Pawing

Urination, especially in puppies

Appeasing: "I just want to be friends."

Submissive

This posture says "I give up. Don't hurt me. You've won." Ignore the dog. When he comes to you, do something he perceives as pleasant—throw a ball or give him a treat.

Stressed

This dog is overloaded. Whatever the situation, it is too much for him. Stop whatever you are doing and remove the dog from the situation.

The more time you spend observing your dog, the better you get at interpreting what's on his mind. Your dog is already an expert, and you can become one, too.

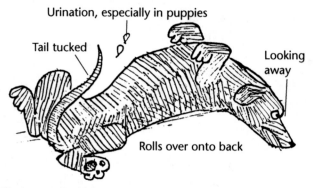

Submissive: "I give up. Don't hurt me. You win."

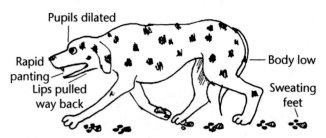

Stressed: "I'm just so overwhelmed."

Laddie learned to open the gate.

HOW YOUR DOG LEARNS

Your dog learns from his everyday experiences, some of which are pleasant, others are not. He also learns to make positive or negative associations with specific behaviors. For example, while pawing at the gate one day, Laddie the Collie accidentally opened it and took himself for a nice long walk in the neighborhood. From then on, whenever he wanted to go for a walk, he would paw at the gate until it opened.

Max the Dachshund did not fare as well. One winter day he was walking near the garage when a huge pile of snow slid off the roof and buried him. He now makes a big arc whenever he walks around the garage.

WHO IS TRAINING WHOM?

Training is a two-way street—Felix is just as involved in training you as you are in training him. Every time you interact with your dog, some form of training takes place. You may not be aware of it at the time, but it will shape his behavior.

Max remembers being buried by the snow.

Your dog has you well trained.

Take the following quiz to find out if your dog is, in fact, training *you*.

What do you do when your dog:

1. Drops a ball in your lap while you are watching television?
2. Nudges or paws your elbow when you are sitting on the couch?
3. Rattles the food dish?
4. Sits at the door?

If your answers are:

1. Throw it.
2. Pet the dog.
3. Fill the dish.
4. Open the door.

. . . then your dog has you well trained!

You are responsible for shaping your dog's behavior.

When Deacon was a puppy, nobody thought anything about slipping him something from the dinner table. Now he is 6 months old, almost fully grown, and he is begging at the table. What happened? He was systematically trained to beg by being given food from the table.

Since his begging has become a nuisance, everyone wants to put a stop to it. The family resolves not to feed him from the table anymore. At first, Deacon does not believe this is happening, and he digs a little deeper into his repertoire of begging routines. Sure enough, someone takes pity on him and slips him a treat.

As this scenario repeats itself, often with longer and longer intervals before someone gives in, Deacon is systematically being trained not to take "no" for an answer and that persistence pays! Looking at it from Deacon's point of view, the family is rewarding, even encouraging, the very behavior it finds objectionable. As soon as they stop giving in to Deacon his efforts will decrease, and over time (and provided they don't have a relapse), he will stop begging altogether. In technical jargon, you have extinguished the undesired behavior by refusing to reward it.

Do not give in!

Good training rewards the desired behavior and discourages or ignores the undesired behavior. Start good training by paying attention to what you are rewarding and ask yourself: Do I really want my dog to do this? Is this something I want to live with as long as I have this dog? If the answers are "no," then stop rewarding these behaviors.

Don't underestimate your dog's ability to train you. Many dogs have done a much better job of training their owners than the other way around.

Facts from Felix

1) Dogs are experts at reading body language.

2) The best time to stop undesirable behavior is when your dog is thinking about it.

3) Discipline after the offending deed is ineffective.

4) Dogs learn through pleasant and unpleasant experiences.

5) Become aware of who is training whom.

6) Good training rewards the desired behavior and discourages or ignores the undesired behavior.

A crate is like having a baby-sitter for your dog.

Chapter 4

A "Baby-sitter" for Your Dog

When Rita and Ted went to pick up their puppy, the breeder asked them what they thought was a peculiar question. "When you were raising your children, did you use a playpen?"

"Of course," said Rita. "I don't know what I would have done without it."

"Fine," said the breeder. "A crate for a puppy is like a playpen for a child."

Whatever your views on playpens, dogs like crates. It reminds them of a den—a place of safety, security, and warmth. Puppies, and many adult dogs, sleep most of the day, and many prefer the comfort of their den.

ADVANTAGES OF A CRATE

For everyone's peace of mind, get a crate for your dog. Here are just a few of the many advantages of crate training your dog:

- When you're busy and can't keep an eye on your puppy Felix, but want to make sure he will not get into trouble, put him in a crate. You can relax, and so can he.

- Crates are ideal for establishing a schedule for housetraining.

- Few dogs are fortunate enough to go through life without ever having to be hospitalized. Your dog's private room at the veterinary hospital will consist of a crate. Felix's first experience with a crate should not come at a time when he is sick, as the added stress from being crated for the first time will slow his recovery. There may also be times when you have to keep your dog confined, such as after an injury or being altered.

 Crating a dog in a vehicle is equally important when you leave him in the car while you run some errands. Fred learned this lesson the hard way. He left Gretchen, his 6-month-old Dachshund, loose in the car for about two hours. By the time he returned, she had done *major* damage to the upholstery!

39

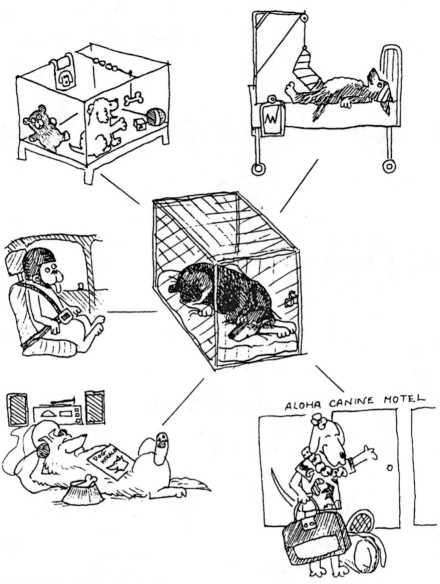

Crate training has many advantages.

- Driving any distance, even around the block, with your dog loose in the car is tempting fate. Imagine what can happen if you have to slam on the brakes for some reason. Having the dog in a crate protects you and your dog. For some vehicles, crates are too large or cumbersome, but it is still just as important to protect your dog while riding in the car. Patty found the answer for her Lab, Bailey—she purchased a harness especially designed for dogs that is attached to a seat belt, not unlike a car seat for a child. In a

Collapsible wire crate

Plastic airline crate

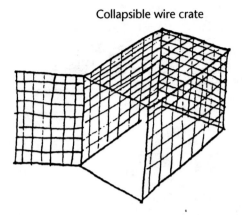
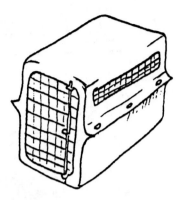

Types of crates.

station wagon or an SUV, another alternative is a dog barrier that separates the cargo area from the main cabin.

• When you go on vacation, you may want to take your dog. A crate is a home away from home, and you can leave Felix in a hotel room knowing that he won't be unhappy or stressed, or try to tear up the room.

• Most important for your dog, the crate is a place where he can get away from the hustle and bustle of family life and hide out when the kids become too much for him.

Your dog will like the crate because it will remind him of the security of a den. He will use it voluntarily, so he should always have access to it. Depending on where it is, your dog will spend a lot of time sleeping in his crate.

SELECTING A CRATE

Select a crate that is large enough so your dog can turn around, stand, or lie down comfortably. Even if the dog is still a puppy, get a crate for the adult-size dog. You will need a divider at first (some crates come with one).

Buy a good-quality crate that collapses easily and is portable so you can take it with you when traveling with your dog. If you frequently take your dog with you in the car, consider getting two crates, one for the house and one for the car, so you don't have to lug one back and forth.

INTRODUCING YOUR DOG TO THE CRATE

Set up the crate and let the puppy investigate it. Choose a command, such as "Crate" or "Go to Bed." Physically place your puppy in the crate using the command you have chosen. Tell him what a great little guy he is, give him a bite-sized treat, and then let him out.

Introduction to the crate.

Next, use a treat to coax him into the crate. If he does not follow the treat, physically place him into the crate and then give him the treat.

Repeat until the puppy goes into the crate with almost no help from you, each time using the command and giving a treat *after* he is in the crate.

If the puppy is afraid of the crate, use his meals to overcome this fear. First, let him eat the meal in front of the crate, and then place the next meal just inside the crate. Put each successive meal a little farther into the crate until he is completely inside and no longer reluctant to go in.

The same procedure is used for introducing an adolescent or adult dog to a crate.

GETTING YOUR DOG USED TO THE CRATE

Follow these steps to get your dog adjusted to the crate. Tell your dog to go into the crate, give him a treat, close the door, and tell him what a good boy he is, and then let him out again. Each time you do this, leave Felix in the crate a little longer with the door closed, still giving a treat and telling him how great he is.

What you see...

What he sees...

Your dog's perception of a crate.

Finally, put him in the crate, give a treat, and then leave the room, first for five minutes, then ten minutes, then fifteen minutes, and so on. Each time you return to let him out, tell Felix how good he is before you open the door.

How long can you ultimately leave your adult dog in a crate unattended? That depends on your dog and your schedule, but ideally it should not be more than three to four hours during the day. Although many dogs seem content to stay in a crate for most of the day while their owners are at work, shorter periods are preferable. Some dog owners who need to crate their pets for long periods are fortunate enough to have a neighbor come in during the day to let the dog out for awhile and give him a chance to stretch his legs and relieve himself (see chapter 5 for specifics on housetraining).

A WORD OF CAUTION

A crate should never be used as a form of punishment. If it is, your dog will begin to dislike the crate, and it will lose its usefulness to you. The old "go to your room without supper" approach does not work any better with dogs than it does with children.

Facts from Felix

1) For everyone's peace of mind, crate-train your dog.

2) A crate reminds your dog of a den.

3) Dogs like the safety and security of a crate.

4) Among its many advantages, a crate is ideal for housetraining.

5) When traveling with your dog in the car, for his safety and yours, put Felix in a crate, or a harness that attaches to the seat belt.

6) A crate is never used as a form of punishment.

Chapter 5

Housetraining

If you plan to keep your dog in the backyard and never let him inside the house, there is no need to housetrain him. But if your dog is going to be a house dog, you need to housetrain him. As with any training, the best time to start is as soon as you get him.

The keys to successful housetraining are:

1. Crate train your puppy or adult dog (see chapter 4).
2. Set a schedule for feeding and exercising your dog.
3. Stick to that schedule, even on weekends, at least until your dog is housetrained and mature.
4. Be vigilant, vigilant, and vigilant until your dog is trained.

Using a crate is the most humane and effective way to housetrain your puppy. It is also the easiest because of the dog's natural desire to keep his den clean.

HOUSETRAINING YOUR PUPPY

Puppies have to eliminate two to three times more frequently than adult dogs in a 24-hour period. A puppy's ability to control elimination increases with age, from not at all to up to eight hours or more. During the day, when active, the puppy can last for only short periods. Until he is 6 months of age, it is unrealistic to expect him to last for more than four hours during the day without having to eliminate. When sleeping, most puppies can last through the night.

Necessary items for housetraining.

If your puppy needs to urinate frequently and has repeated accidents in the house, she may have cystitis, an infection that requires a visit to the veterinarian. Cystitis is more common in female puppies than male puppies.

Setting a schedule

Dogs and puppies thrive on a regular routine. By feeding and exercising your dog at about the same time every day, your pup will also relieve himself at about the same time every day.

Set a time to feed the puppy that is convenient for you. Always feed at the same time. Until 4 months of age, a puppy needs four meals a day; from 5 to 7 months, three meals. From then on feed twice a day—it is healthier than feeding only once a day and helps with housetraining.

Stick to the schedule.

FEEDING SCHEDULE

Age	Feed
7 through 16 weeks	four times a day
17 through 28 weeks	three times a day
29 weeks and over	two times a day

Feed the right amount—loose stools are a sign of overfeeding; straining or dry stools are a sign of underfeeding. After ten minutes, pick up the food dish and put it away. Do not have food available at other times. Keep the diet constant—abrupt diet changes can cause digestive upsets that will hinder your housetraining efforts.

Fresh water must be available to your dog during the day. You can put away the water dish after 8:00 P.M. so the pup can last through the night.

Establishing a toilet area

Start by selecting a toilet area and always go to that spot when you want your dog to eliminate. If possible, pick a place in a straight line from the house. Carry your puppy or put him on leash. Stand still so the dog can concentrate on eliminating. Teach a command, such as "Hurry Up." The command, which he will learn in time, is used to encourage the pup to eliminate quickly. Still, you need to be patient and let the pup sniff around. After he is done, lavishly praise your puppy and go back inside.

First thing in the morning, Mary takes her 12-week-old Poodle puppy, Colette, out of the crate and straight outside to the toilet area. Fifteen minutes after Colette's morning meal, she is let out again. Mary then crates Colette and leaves for work.

On her lunch break, Mary goes home to let Colette out to relieve herself, feeds her, and then, just to make sure, takes her out once more. For the afternoon, Colette is crated again until

> There are three rules dog lovers and non-dog lovers agree on: One, you need to pick up after your dog on public or someone else's property; two, don't permit your dog to jump on other people; and three, don't let your dog bark incessantly. Be a good dog neighbor and follow these rules.

Mary returns. Colette is then walked and fed, after which she spends the rest of the evening in the house where Mary can keep an eye on her. Before bedtime, Mary takes Colette to the toilet area once more and then crates her for the night.

Sample schedule.

When Colette turns 7 months old, Mary will drop the noontime feeding and walk. From then on, most dogs only need to go out immediately or soon after waking up in the morning, in the late afternoon, and once again before bedtime.

Being vigilant

Take your puppy to his toilet area after eating or drinking, after waking up, and after playing. A sign that your dog has to go out is sniffing the ground and circling in a small area.

Circling

Eating or drinking

Playing

Sleeping

Take your puppy out after . . .

Special vigilance is required when it is raining because many dogs, particularly those with short hair, do not like to go out in the wet any more than you do. Make sure the puppy actually eliminates before you bring him back into the house.

DEALING WITH ACCIDENTS

When your dog has had an accident in the house, *do not* call him to you to punish him. It is too late. If you do punish your dog under these circumstances, it will not help your housetraining efforts and you will make the dog wary of wanting to come to you.

There is a popular misconception that Felix "knows" what he did because he looks "guilty." *Absolutely not so.* He has that look because he knows from prior experience that when you come across a mess, you get angry. Your dog has learned to associate a mess with your angry response. He cannot make the connection between making the mess in the first place and your anger.

Swatting your dog with a rolled-up newspaper is cruel and only creates fear of you and rolled-up newspapers. Rubbing the dog's nose in the mess is unsanitary and disgusting. Dogs become housetrained in spite of such tactics, not because of them.

When you come upon an accident, always keep calm. Put Felix out of sight so he cannot watch you clean up—observing you cleaning up stimulates some dogs to eliminate at that same spot again. Use white vinegar as a cleaner or you can buy a special cleaner designed to remove the smell of urine. Do not use ammonia-based cleaners because the ammonia does not neutralize the odor, so the puppy will still be attracted to the same place.

Catching your dog in the act

If you catch your dog in the act, sharply clap your hands. If the dog stops, take him to his toilet area. If he doesn't, try to stay calm. Whatever you do, do not attempt to drag him outside; that will make your cleanup job that much more difficult.

Regression

Regression *will* occur, especially during teething. Regression well after 6 months of age may be a sign that your dog is ill. If accidents persist, visit your veterinarian.

 Until your puppy is reliable, keep an eye on him and watch for signs that he may have to go out, especially sniffing in a circling motion. When you are not able to supervise him, put him in his crate.

Facts from Felix

1) Using a crate to housetrain your puppy is the most humane and effective way.

2) When active, puppies can last only short periods before they have to eliminate.

3) Dogs thrive on a regular routine of feeding and exercising at the same time every day.

4) It is healthier for an adult dog to be fed twice a day rather than once a day.

5) Take your puppy to his toilet area after waking up, after eating or drinking, and after playing or chewing.

6) When your dog has had an accident in the house, do not call him to you and then punish him.

DOGS

Chapter 6

Sit and Stay

Dogs have perfected different styles of greetings. Bart the Lab would launch himself about 6 feet toward his owner, who did not appreciate having to catch this missile at every greeting. Other dogs jump on people to greet them, which most people find annoying, even people who have dogs. And don't believe the line "It's okay—I don't mind." Nor does the size of the dog matter—a Yorkshire Terrier can ruin a pair of nylons just as quickly as a larger dog. For these antics, the Sit and Stay is the answer.

JUMPING ON PEOPLE

The question almost every dog owner asks is "How do I keep my dog from jumping on people?"

Dogs jump on people as a form of greeting, like saying "Hello, nice to meet you!" Even the briefest of separations from the owner, as little as five minutes, can set off this behavior.

As annoying as it may be at times, please remember that this greeting is a gesture of affection and goodwill. We certainly do not recommend any form of punishment to deal with it.

So how do you get your dog to stop jumping on people without dampening his enthusiasm? By teaching him to Sit and Stay on command. Your dog can't jump on you when he is sitting—the two behaviors are mutually exclusive.

In polite company, the Sit and Stay commands are essential.

Greeting behavior when untrained.

SAFETY

Equally annoying, but far more dangerous, is the dog's habit of dashing through doors just because they are open. It is dangerous because he may find himself in the middle of the road and get hit by a car, or, if you are in the process of opening a door, he may knock you down as he rushes through.

Teaching your dog to Sit and Stay while you open the door and to wait until you indicate that he can go out can prevent such potential accidents.

Sit and Stay also applies to getting in and out of the car as well as going up and down stairs. Having both arms full while going down a staircase with a dog dashing by is not a good idea.

When the doorbell rings, you can tell your dog to "Sit" and "Stay" while you answer it instead of having him frantically charge toward the door.

All these maneuvers can be performed smoothly and without worry, once you have taught your dog to Sit and Stay.

 The Sit and Stay is one of the simplest and most useful exercises you can teach your dog. It gives you a wonderfully easy way to control your pet when you need it most.

Use Sit and Stay when you want your dog to remain quietly in one spot for a *short* time. For example, Keno, a German Shepherd, would become so excited when Sally was about to feed him that he would send the dish flying out of her hands. Once taught the Sit and Stay, he sat like a perfect gentleman while she put his dish down and he calmly waited until she released him.

The Sit and Stay commands are important for safety.

COMMANDS TO BE TAUGHT

You are going to teach your dog three commands:

1. Sit
2. Stay
3. OK

"OK" is the release command. It means Felix can move now and do whatever he wants (almost). Make sure you give the release command *every time* after you have told Felix to stay to indicate that he is now allowed to move again. Should you get lax about it and forget, Felix will get into the habit of releasing himself and learn that *he* can decide when to move, the opposite of what *you* want.

Unless impaired, a dog's sense of hearing is extremely acute, so when giving a command there is no need to shout. Give commands such as "Sit!" in a normal tone of voice. Note that "Sit!" is a command, not a question. The release word "OK" is given in a more excited tone of voice, to convey, "That's it, you're all done for now."

When teaching a new command, you may have to repeat it several times before your dog catches on. When you are past that initial stage, teach Felix to respond to the *first* command. Give the command, and if nothing happens, show your dog exactly what you want by physically helping him. Consistency is the key to success.

Teaching your dog the Sit command

Your dog already knows how to sit. But he has to learn what you expect from him when you say "Sit" and to obey every time you give him the command.

Begin by showing Felix a small, bite-sized treat, holding it just a little in front of his eyes and slightly over his head. (By using a small, bite-sized treat of something very tasty, the dog will remain interested in his reward and will work hard to get it. If your dog seems bored with the treat, try another type of goodie or make the treats smaller so he doesn't get full so quickly.) Say "Sit" as you bring your hand above his eyes. Looking up at the treat will ease your dog into a sitting position. When he does, give him the treat and tell him what a good puppy he is. Tell him without petting him. If you pet as you praise him, he will probably get up when you really want him to sit.

Study the illustration on the next page for the position of your hand in relation to your dog's head. If you hold your hand too high, your dog will jump up; if it is too low, he will not sit.

If after several attempts Felix does not respond, physically show him what you want him to do by placing him into a sit as follows: With your dog standing at your left side, both of you facing in the same direction, kneel on your right knee, put the thumb of your right hand through his collar under his chin, fingers on his chest, pointing down. Place your left hand on top of his shoulder, then slide it down his back, all the way under the tail to the back of his legs, apply equal pressure with the right hand against his chest and the left hand against his back legs and gently tuck him into a sit, saying "Sit" as you do so. Verbally praise, keep your hands in position to the count of five, and then release your dog.

Practice having your dog sit five times in a row for five days. Some dogs catch on to this idea so quickly that whenever they want a treat they sit in front of their owner.

When Felix understands what "Sit" means, you can start to teach him to obey your command. Put your hand through his collar at the top of the neck, palm facing up, and tell him to "Sit." If he does, give him a treat and tell him how good he is; if he does not, pull up on the collar, wait until he sits, and praise and reward with a treat.

Teaching the Sit command.

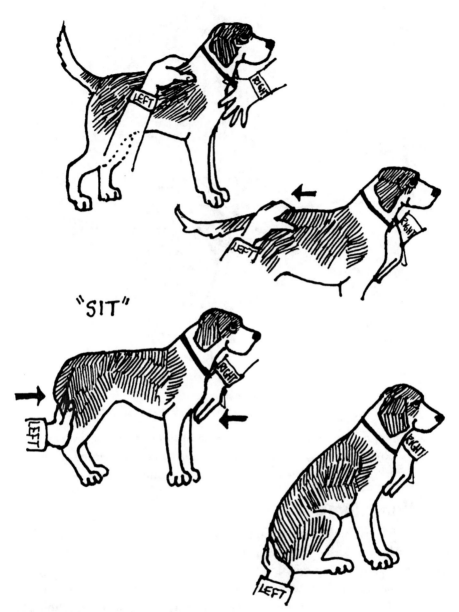

"SIT"

Placing your dog into a sit.

Practice until he sits on command—that is, without you having to pull up on or touch the collar. Give a treat and praise with "Good puppy" for *every* correct response.

When he sits on command *only*, reward the desired response every other time. Finally, reward on a random basis—every now and then give a treat after he sits

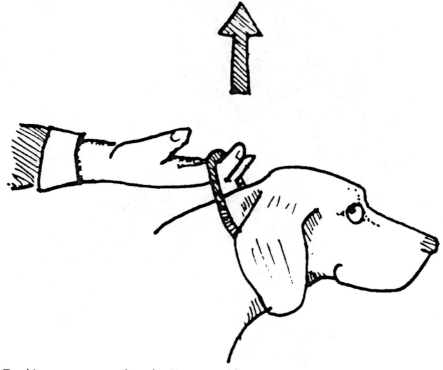

Teaching your pup to obey the Sit command.

on command. A random reward is the most powerful reinforcement of what your dog has learned. It is based on the simple premise that hope springs eternal. To make it work, all you have to do is use it and keep using it!

Sit, don't jump

Now, when Felix wants to greet you by jumping up, tell him to "Sit." Bend down, briefly pet him and tell him what a good puppy he is, and then release him by saying "OK." By following this simple method consistently, you will change your dog's greeting behavior from trying to jump on you to sitting to be petted.

A dog's habit of jumping on visitors is handled in a similar way, although it requires a helper. All the initial training is done on leash until Felix can be trusted off leash. Ask a friend or neighbor to visit and have Felix sit at your left side. Should he get up as your helper comes inside, reinforce the Sit. Instruct your helper to avoid eye contact with Felix and to ignore him.

Have your helper sit on a chair and tell him to ignore Felix. Then let Felix off leash and see what he does. Should he try to climb up on your helper, take Felix by the collar, and say, "Sit," followed by "Stay." Then tell your helper to leave. After he has left, release Felix with "OK."

Use helpers to practice the Sit and Stay at the door.

Repeat this procedure several times, preferably with different helpers, until Felix understands he is not to jump on guests. The important part is that the helper ignores the dog—any interaction, such as eye contact between your helper and Felix, will cause Felix to want to go to your helper.

Can the helper ever say "Hello" to the dog and pet him? Of course he can, once Felix has been trained to ignore the helper, and as long as Felix remains in a Sit and Stay when your helper says "Hello" and pets him.

Sitting for supper

An easy way to teach your dog to understand the Stay command is to make him sit and stay for his meals. As you are getting ready to feed him, bowl in hand, say, "Sit," followed by "Stay," and lower the bowl to the ground. As your pup starts for it, pick up the bowl before he gets even a mouthful. Put him back where he was supposed to sit and stay. Start all over. Repeat until you can put the bowl down and count to five before saying "OK." Then let him eat in peace.

If your dog is very bouncy or excitable, you may want to put him on leash for better control. (For leash training, see chapter 9.) Fold the leash into your left hand short enough so you

The closer to your dog's collar you hold the leash, the more control you have of the dog. Hold the leash in such a way that the part that goes to the dog comes out at the bottom (below your pinky) part of your hand.

Before and after learning the Sit command.

can control your dog. Tell him to "Sit" and "Stay" and start to put his bowl across the floor. If he moves, pull up on the leash and wait until he sits. You may have to try this a few times until he gets the message.

After several days of following this regimen, your dog will sit on his own when he sees you approaching with his dish and wait until you say "OK." This is a much more pleasant way to feed your dog than having him jump up and down, trying to knock the dish out of your hands.

Door manners

Once he will sit and stay for food, you are ready for the next important lesson: Wait until you tell him "OK" *before* he dashes through that door. Start by sitting your dog in front of a closed door. You know that if you open the door, Felix will want to go through. Tell him to "Stay" and start opening the door. When he starts to get up, close the door, put him back in the exact spot where you said "Stay," and start over.

If your dog is particularly fast or very strong, use a leash the same way you used it to teach him to sit for supper. With your dog on a Stay, practice until you can open the door all the way before closing it again.

Praise is verbal, such as "Good dog" when Felix obeys a command, but it is not an invitation to move. The release means "OK, you are done with that particular exercise and can now move."

Teaching the Stay command.

You will find that after three or four repetitions, Felix gets the message and will stay. Since he wants to go out, he learns it is to his advantage to stay until you say the magic word. From now on, every time you let Felix out, make him sit first, open the door, and then release with "OK." Get into the habit of having your dog sit and stay before you open any door.

Some people prefer to go through the doorway before the dog, whereas others want the dog to go through first. It makes no difference, so long as Felix stays until you release him. Practice with the doors your dog uses regularly, *including the car doors*. Teach Felix to stay in the car as you open the door, put on his leash, and then let him out with "OK." Every time you make him sit and stay, it reinforces your position as pack leader and that you are the one in charge.

Staying for stairs

If you have stairs, start teaching your dog to stay at the bottom while you go up. First sit him, and then give the Stay command. When he tries to follow, put him back and start again. Practice until you can go all the way up the stairs with him waiting at the bottom before you release him to follow. Repeat the same procedure going down the stairs.

Practical applications of the Sit command.

Once your dog has been trained to wait at one end of the stairs, you will discover that he will anticipate the release. He will jump the gun and get up just as you are thinking of releasing him. Before long, he will stay only briefly and release when *he* chooses. It may happen almost as soon as he has grasped the idea, or it may take a few weeks or even months, but it *will* happen.

When it does, stop whatever you are doing and put him back, count to ten, and then release. *Do not let him get into the habit of releasing himself.* Consistency is just as important here as in any other exercise.

Facts from Felix

1) Sit and Stay is used when you want your dog to remain quietly in one spot for a short time.

2) When your dog sits on command, he cannot jump on you.

3) Sit and Stay applies to going through doors, up and down stairs, and in and out of the car.

4) A random reward is the most powerful reinforcement of what your dog has learned.

5) After you have given the Stay command, remember to release — make it a strict rule.

6) Unless you periodically reinforce the Stay, your dog will begin to release himself.

This dog needs to learn the Go Lie Down command.

Chapter 7

Go Lie Down

Now that your dog responds to "Sit," he is ready for the next lesson: to lie down on command.

You are going to teach Felix two new commands:

1. Down.
2. Go Lie Down.

You use "Down" when you want Felix to lie down in place right now and stay there until you give the release command.

You use "Go Lie Down" when you want him to remain quietly in one place for a long time, from five minutes up to one hour. The command is most commonly used when you are eating or when friends visit and you don't want your dog making a pest of himself. When you give the command, he is expected to go to a favorite spot and get comfortable. Release him when you are ready for him to get up again.

TEACHING YOUR DOG TO LIE DOWN ON COMMAND

Of course, your dog already knows how to lie down. What you are going to teach him is to do it when *you* tell him.

First, sit your dog at your left side. Put two fingers of your left hand, palm facing you, through the collar at the side of his neck. Have a treat in your right hand. Show him the treat directly in front of his nose, say "Down," and lower the treat

Teaching the Down command.

straight down and in front of your dog as you apply a little downward pressure on the collar. When he lies down, give him the treat and praise by telling him quietly what a good puppy he is. Keep your left hand in the collar and your right hand off your puppy while telling him how clever he is so he learns to be praised for lying down. Petting your dog as a form of praise will get him all excited and he will forget what you wanted him to do.

Reverse the process by showing Felix a treat in front of his nose and bringing it up slightly above his head with a little upward tension on the collar as you tell him to "Sit."

In the following illustration, study the way the right hand moves down and in front of your dog in an L shape, and the position of the left hand. Place the treat between the dog's front legs so he learns to lie down in place and without moving forward.

With a small dog, it is easier to teach the Down on a table than on the floor. You'll need a sturdy table and a nonslip surface such as a bathtub mat so your dog does not slip on the table.

Some dogs don't respond to a treat. This seeming lack of interest happens when the treat is vaguely waived somewhere in the vicinity of the dog's head, instead of directly in front of his nose. Another reason could be that the dog is not interested in that particular treat. You need to experiment with what works best for your dog. (Stay away from treats containing a lot of sugar or salt, which are unhealthy for your dog.)

Other dogs are just not sufficiently interested in food. If your dog won't lie down for a treat or other object of attraction, such as a toy, you can physically place him into the down position and then praise or reward him with a treat. (An object of attraction is anything your dog will actively work for.)

To place Felix in the down position, place him into a sit at your left side. Kneel next to him, with both of you facing the same direction. With your left hand reach over his back and pick up his left foreleg with the palm of your hand, keeping your thumb pointing straight up. Place your right hand behind his right foreleg with your thumb pointing up. Say "Down" as you *lift* and *lower* your dog down. Praise and keep your hands *still* to a count of five. If you apply pressure on your dog's forelegs with your thumbs, he will try to pull away from you and you will find yourself in a wrestling match with your dog. Not a good idea!

For the particularly squirmy dog, place your left forearm firmly against his left side as you place him into the down position.

Practice having your dog lie down at your side five times in a row for five days, or until he does it on command and without you having to touch his collar. Verbally praise him and reward with a treat every time.

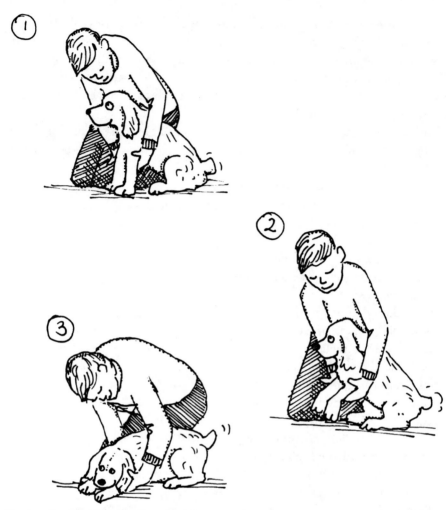

Placing the dog into the down position.

When he understands what the Down command means, you can move on to the next step. Sit your dog at your left side and put two fingers of your left hand, palm facing you, through the collar at the side of his neck. Say "Down" and apply slight downward pressure on the collar. When your dog lies down, *slowly* take your hand out of the collar, praise, and give him a treat every *other* time. Practice over the course of several days until he will lie down on command without you having to touch his collar.

After that, when he lies down on command, randomly reward as explained in chapter 6.

Practice the response to the Down command.

TEACHING YOUR DOG TO REMAIN IN PLACE

You can now teach your dog to lie down in one place for several minutes. Sit in a chair and have your dog sit at your left side. Say "Down" and apply a little pressure on the collar. Keep an eye on him, and when he tries to get up, place him down again. Teach him to stay in the down position for five minutes, and then praise and release with "OK."

If your dog is very bouncy, you may want to put him on a leash and then sit on the leash so your hands are free to put him back into the down position.

As he learns to stay in the down position, gradually and over the course of several sessions increase the time he will stay to thirty minutes before you release. This sounds boring and time-consuming, but you can read or watch TV while he is doing his down.

There is no need to tell your dog to stay since "Down" or "Go Lie Down" includes "stay until released." But you do have to remember to release your dog with an "OK" so he does not just get up at will, which would defeat the object of the exercise.

Be persistent when teaching a dog to remain in the down position.

TEACHING THE GO LIE DOWN COMMAND

"Go Lie Down" is a useful command when you want Felix to go to a specific spot and remain there for an extended period until you release him. Use this command whenever you don't want Felix underfoot, such as at mealtimes or when you have visitors and don't want him making a pest of himself.

Select the spot where you want Felix to hang out—his crate, bed, favorite chair, whatever. You can also select an object that is easily moved to different locations, such as a blanket, crate pad, or a slightly raised dog bed. Assume you're going to use a dog bed. Start by taking your dog to the bed and telling him "Go Lie Down." You may have to coax him with a treat. When he lies down on the bed, verbally praise, give him the treat, count to five, and release him. Repeat until he readily lies down on the bed.

Next, stand three feet from the bed, give the command "Go Lie Down," and lure him onto the bed with a treat. Praise him when he lies down, give him the treat, count to ten, and release him. Repeat several times, gradually increasing the time between the praise and the giving of the treat, from a count of ten to a count of thirty. Stop for now—you're getting bored and so is Felix—and come back to it at another time.

Teaching the Go Lie Down command.

For your next session, review the last progression two or three times and send Felix from three feet away. Stand still, toss a treat onto the bed, say "Go Lie Down," and motion him to go to his bed. He may surprise you and actually go to his bed and lie down. If he does, praise him enthusiastically. If he just stands there with a befuddled look on his face, put one finger through his collar, gently guide him to his bed, and have him lie down. You may have to repeat this process several times until he responds to the command.

Repeat until Felix responds reliably from three feet, with you still tossing the treat onto the bed. Now try sending him without tossing the treat first. When he responds correctly, praise, go to him, and give him a treat. If he stands there like a bump on a log, take him by the collar, calmly guide him to the bed, have him lie down, and verbally praise.

When he reliably goes to his bed from three feet, gradually over the course of several sessions, increase the distance from the bed, as well as the length of time—up to thirty minutes—you want him to stay there. If he gets up without being released, just put him back (put your finger through the collar and lead him back). Reward him with a treat on a random basis.

The Go Lie Down command, although practical, isn't the most exciting exercise. Use common sense and don't make it drudgery. Maintain an upbeat attitude and keep the actual training sessions (the number of times you send him to his place) short. Several short sessions during the course of a day are better than one long session.

Once he understands what is expected, make sure he responds to the first command of "Go Lie Down" that you give. If he doesn't, stop what you are doing and place him on his bed.

Facts from Felix

1)   Down is another exercise that teaches your dog that you are in charge.

2)   Down is used when you want him to lie down in place, right now.

3)   Go Lie Down is used when you want your dog to remain quietly in one place for long periods of time.

4)   Remember to keep your thumbs up when placing the dog into the Down position.

5)   Be sure you release the dog so that he doesn't get into the habit of releasing himself at will.

6)   Reward correct responses on a random basis.

Chapter 8

Walking Your Dog

Taking your dog for a nice long walk is a balm for the soul and good exercise for both of you, provided your dog does not drag you down the street.

Even if you and your dog don't ordinarily go for walks, teaching your pet some manners while on leash is still a good idea. For example, at least once a year you

Walking on leash is necessary at the vet.

Some puppies balk at going away from the house, in which case you just pick him up, carry him some way from the house, and let him walk back. Before you know it, he will not only walk on the leash in your direction, but actually pull you along.

will have to go to the veterinarian. If your dog has been trained to walk on leash, the visit will go much more smoothly than if Felix bounces off the end of the leash like a kangaroo. (Of course, if the dog is small, you can always carry him, but you should still get a small dog used to walking on leash.)

Most people want to be able to take their dog for a walk within the length of the leash without pulling. A leisurely stroll is an important daily routine, and for many dogs the only opportunity to get some fresh air.

LEASH-TRAINING YOUR DOG

Before you can start the section on teaching Felix not to pull, you need to get him accustomed to wearing a collar and walking on a leash.

From your local pet-supply store, purchase an adjustable buckle collar of fabric or leather. Take your puppy's neck measurement before you go. The collar should be snug, about as snug as a turtleneck sweater, high on the neck and just behind the ears, so that he cannot back out of it or catch it on anything. As Felix grows, you may have to buy a larger collar.

For your leash choose five-eighths-inch-wide cotton web or leather, six feet in length. Either one will hold even the largest of dogs. The least desirable leash is one made of chain—it is extremely uncomfortable on your hands.

Fasten the collar around Felix's neck and see what he does. Most puppies show little reaction to a collar. Some will scratch their neck at first, but as they become accustomed to wearing the collar, they ignore it.

When he is used to his collar, attach the leash and let him drag it around. You will need to supervise him so that he does not get tangled. Once he ignores the leash, pick up the other end and follow him around. He will happily wander off wherever his fancy takes him.

You are now ready to show him where you want to go. First use a treat to make him follow you and then gently guide him with the leash, telling him what a good puppy he is. If you are teaching outside, use the treat to coax him away from the house and the leash to guide him back toward the house.

TEACHING YOUR DOG NOT TO PULL

The ultimate goal of training your dog not to pull is to teach him to pay attention to you. To accomplish this goal, you need to train yourself to pay attention to your dog.

To teach Felix not to pull, you need his collar, your leash, and a few treats. Decide where you want him to walk in relation to you—the traditional position is at your left side.

How seriously you approach training will depend on how often you plan taking Felix for a walk and for what purpose. If you like to take him along while you jog or go for a brisk walk, then he has to learn to stay at your side so you don't trip over him. If you walk only so that he can relieve himself, it matters little where he is in relation to you, so long as he does not pull.

Go to an area without too many distractions (such as other people and dogs, especially loose dogs) and where you can walk in a straight line for about fifty feet or a circle about thirty feet in diameter.

Put the loop of the leash over the thumb of your right hand and make a fist around the leash. Place your left hand on the leash directly under your right hand

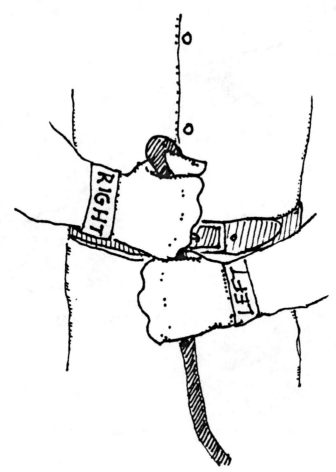

Holding the leash.

as though you are holding a baseball bat. Place both hands against your belt buckle and firmly hold them there.

Say "Let's go" and start walking. When Felix gets ahead of you and begins to pull on the leash, stop! When he stops pulling and looks back at you to see what the holdup is, say "Good dog," and if he actually comes to you to check in with you, give him a treat, then continue walking.

For your next training session, practice the "stop and go" procedure several times. After this review, start to walk again, except this time just before Felix gets

Dogs need to pay attention to where the owner is going.

to the end of the leash, say "Let's go," make a right about-face in the opposite direction and continue walking, keeping your hands firmly locked in place. When Felix catches up with you and *looks* at you, tell him what a good boy he is and give him a treat.

When you make your about-face, Felix experiences a tug on the leash, telling him he has to pay attention to you. Anticipate when Felix is going to pull and

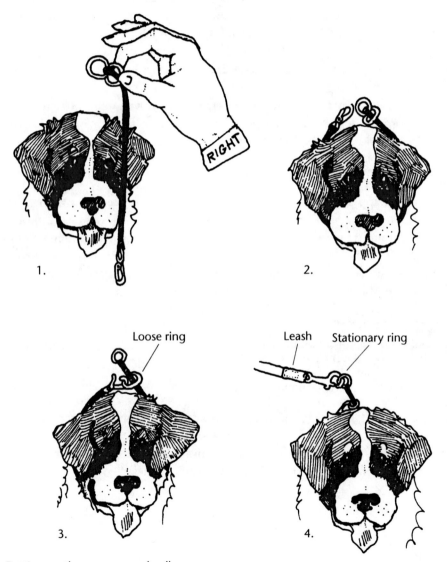

Putting on the snap-around collar.

make your turn *before* the leash tightens. Once the leash tightens, you are in a pulling match with your dog—and guess who is going to win.

When Felix turns toward you without any tension on the leash after you say "Let's go," praise him enthusiastically and give him a treat.

The two of you are now ready for the next step—to teach Felix to pay attention to where *you* are going. Begin as before, only this time start making turns without giving Felix a command. You are teaching him it is his responsibility to pay attention to you and not the other way around. The first few times he will experience a tug on the leash, but he will quickly catch on—dogs have amazing peripheral vision. Dogs can also multitask—just because Felix is feverishly sniffing the ground detecting who was there and when, does not mean he is not aware of what you are doing.

You are now ready to take Felix to a new location, one with some distractions. Of course, for your dog, any new area is a distraction. At first, you may find that you have to remind Felix occasionally to pay attention to you by making an about-face.

STILL NOT GETTING IT?

If your dog appears to be particularly dense about the concept of walking on a loose leash, there are several factors to consider. The most obvious one is the area where you are training and the kind of distractions your dog encounters. For example, for most dogs a grass or natural surface is far more distracting than a man-made surface such as asphalt or cement. Moving objects, such as joggers or bicycles, are also more of a distraction to some dogs than others.

> Any kind of training collar is to be used *only* when walking or training your dog. It should be removed from the dog at all other times.

Many dogs do not respond to a buckle collar and need a training collar (also known as a "choke" collar). Traditionally, training collars are made of metal chain and need to be large enough to go over the dog's head. The collar we use is made of nylon and has a snap on one end so that it can be placed around the dog's neck for a proper fit instead of having to go over his head. It is available only by mail order from www.handcraftcollars.com.

Facts from Felix

1) If you want your dog to pay attention to you, you need to pay attention to your dog.

2) How seriously you approach training will depend on how often you plan on taking the dog for a walk.

3) Use a treat and verbal praise when the dog does something correctly.

4) Be patient and maintain a friendly and positive attitude toward your dog.

5) Teach your dog it is his responsibility to pay attention to you.

6) If you can't seem to get anywhere, consider a training collar.

The joy of owning a dog who comes when called.

Chapter 9

Coming When Called

One of the greatest joys of owning a dog is to go for a walk in the park or the woods and let him run, knowing he will come when called. A dog who does not come when called is a prisoner of the leash and, if loose, a danger to himself and others.

If your dog does not come when called, you don't have a good dog!

RULE 1: EXERCISE, EXERCISE, EXERCISE

Many dogs do not come when called because they do not get enough exercise. At every chance, they run off and make the most of it by staying out for hours at a time.

Consider what your dog was bred to do, and that will tell you how much exercise he needs. Just putting Felix out in the backyard will not do. You have to participate. Think of it this way: Exercise is as good for you as it is for your dog.

RULE 2: BE NICE TO YOUR DOG WHEN HE COMES TO YOU

One of the quickest ways to teach your dog *not* to come to you is to call him for punishment or to do something the dog perceives as unpleasant. Most dogs consider being given a bath or a pill unpleasant. When Felix needs either, go and get him instead of calling him to you.

Another example of teaching your dog not to come is to take him for a run in the park and then call him to you when it's time to go home. Repeating this sequence several times teaches the dog "The party's over!" Soon, Felix may become reluctant to return to you when called because he is not ready to end the fun.

Exercise needs vary.

You can prevent this kind of unintentional training by calling your dog to you several times during the outing, sometimes giving a treat, sometimes just a pat on the head. Then let him romp again.

RULE 3: TEACH YOUR DOG TO COME WHEN CALLED AS SOON AS YOU BRING HIM HOME

Ideally, you acquired your dog as a puppy, and that is the best time to teach him to come when called. Start right away.

Sometime between 4 and 8 months of age, your puppy will begin to realize that there is a big, wide world out there, so it may take him longer to come when called. While going through this stage, keep the pup on leash so that he does not learn to ignore you when you call.

RULE 4: WHEN IN DOUBT, KEEP YOUR DOG ON LEASH

Learn to anticipate when your dog is likely *not* to come. You may be tempting fate trying to call once he has spotted a cat, another dog, or a jogger. Of course, there will be times when you goof and let him off leash just as another dog appears out of nowhere.

If your dog dislikes baths, go and get him, but don't call him to you.

Resist the urge to make a complete fool of yourself by bellowing "Come" a million times. The more often you holler "Come," the quicker he learns to ignore you when he is off leash. Instead, patiently go to him and put him on leash. Do not get angry once you have caught him or you will make him afraid; then he will run away when you try to catch him the next time.

RULE 5: ALWAYS TOUCH HIS COLLAR *BEFORE* YOU REWARD WITH A TREAT OR PRAISE

Touching the collar prevents the dog from developing the annoying habit of playing the game of *keep away*—coming toward you and then dancing around you, just out of reach.

THE GAME OF COMING WHEN CALLED

The purpose of the Recall Game is to teach your dog the Come command and to train him to respond reliably to the command. Needed: two people, one hungry dog, one six-foot leash, and plenty of small treats. Here are the steps:

1. Inside the house, with your dog on a six-foot leash, you and your training partner sit on the floor six feet apart and facing each other. Your partner gently hangs on to the dog and you hold the end of the leash. Call your

When in doubt, keep your dog on leash.

dog by saying "Felix, Come," and use the leash to guide the pup to you. Put one hand through the collar under his chin, palm facing up, give a treat, and pet and praise him enthusiastically. (For coming to you, petting is recommended.) To get his attention, the dog's name is always used first before the command is given.

Now you hold the dog and pass the leash to your partner, who says "Felix, Come," guides the dog in, puts a hand through the collar, gives a treat, and pets and praises the dog.

Goal: Repeat until your dog responds voluntarily to being called and no longer needs to be guided with the leash.

2. Repeat step 1 with your dog off leash.

    Goal: Gradually increase the distance between you and your partner to twelve feet.

3. Have your partner hold your dog (off leash) while you hide from Felix (go into another room), then call him. When he finds you, put your hand through the collar, give a treat, and pet and praise. If he can't find you, go to him, take him by his collar, and bring him to the spot where you called. Reward and praise. Now have your partner hide and then call the dog.

    Goal: Repeat until the dog doesn't hesitate in finding you or your partner in any room of the house.

Coming to you doesn't have to be the end of the fun.

GOING OUTSIDE

Take your dog outside to a confined area, such as a fenced yard, tennis court, park, or schoolyard, and repeat steps 1, 2, and 3 of the Recall Game.

You are now ready to practice by yourself. Let Felix loose in a confined area and ignore him. When he is not paying any attention to you, call. When he gets to you, give a treat and make a big fuss. If he does not come, go to him, take his collar, and bring him to the spot where you called and then reward and praise him. Repeat until Felix comes to you every time you call.

The Recall Game—step1.

Once your dog is trained, you don't have to reward with a treat every time, but keep doing so on a random basis.

ADDING DISTRACTIONS

Some dogs need to be trained to come in the face of distractions such as other dogs, children, joggers, food, or friendly strangers. Think about the most irresistible situations for your dog and then practice under those circumstances. Keep in mind that there is no point in increasing the level of difficulty until your dog understands what he is supposed to do in an environment relatively free of distractions.

Increasing the level of difficulty

Now that Felix knows what the Come command means, he needs to learn that he has to respond to it reliably. Knowing a command and obeying it are not the same.

1. Put your dog on a twelve-foot leash (this can be two six-foot leashes tied together or just a piece of rope) and go to an area where you are likely to encounter his favorite distraction (jogger, bicyclist, other dog, whatever). Once he's distracted, let him become thoroughly engrossed, either by watching or straining at the leash, and give the command "Felix, Come." More than likely, he will ignore you. Give a sharp tug on the leash and guide him back to you. Praise him enthusiastically.

   Goal: Repeat three times per session until the dog turns and comes to you immediately when you call. If he does not, you may have to get a snap-around training collar (see chapter 8).

2. Repeat step 1 in different locations with as many different distractions as you can find. Try it with someone offering your dog a tidbit as a distraction

The Recall Game—step 2.

(the dog should not get the treat), someone petting the dog, and anything else that may distract him. Use your imagination.

Goal: A dog who comes immediately when called, even when distracted.

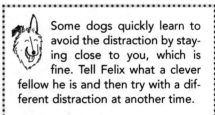 Some dogs quickly learn to avoid the distraction by staying close to you, which is fine. Tell Felix what a clever fellow he is and then try with a different distraction at another time.

The final test

Take your dog to an area where you are not likely to encounter distractions in the form of other dogs or people. Remove the leash and let Felix become involved in smelling the grass or a tree. Keep the distance between you and him about ten feet. Call him. If he responds, pet and praise enthusiastically. If not, avoid the temptation to call him again. Don't worry; he heard you, but chose to ignore you. Instead, slowly walk up behind him, firmly take the collar under his chin, palm up, and trot backward to the spot from where you called. Then praise.

Once Felix is reliable at this point, try an area with other distractions. If he does not respond, practice for the correct response with the twelve-foot leash before you try off leash again.

Can you now trust him to come in an unconfined area? That will depend on how well you have done your homework and what your dog may encounter in the

On-leash distractions.

real world. Understanding your dog and what interests him will help you know when he is not likely to respond to being called.

Let common sense be your guide. For example, when you are traveling and have to let your dog out at a busy interstate rest stop, it is foolhardy to do so off leash. Remember the rule: When in doubt, keep the leash on.

Off-leash distractions.

Use common sense; keep your dog on leash when near the highway.

Facts from Felix

1) If your dog does not come when called, you don't have a good dog.

2) Whenever your dog comes to you, be nice to him.

3) When in doubt, keep the leash on.

4) Always put one hand through the collar after your dog comes to you and before you give a reward.

5) Start now to teach your dog to come when called.

6) "Come" is the most important command you will teach your dog.

Chapter 10

Leave It

When we take our dogs for their daily walk, we are not too thrilled when one of them finds something disgusting he or she perceives to be edible. Nor are we fond of having to extricate such delicacies from a dog's mouth. To tell you the truth, we would prefer if they did not pick up *anything* unknown, potentially edible or not, from the ground. The Leave It command is a good start for controlling such situations.

Owners prefer their dogs not pick up anything unknown from the ground.

Aside from its obvious usefulness, we like teaching this command because it is a wonderful opportunity to learn more about how your dog's thought processes work. As you are teaching him the command your dog will also show you how clever he is at training you. Depending on how quickly Felix catches on, you may want to practice this exercise over the course of several sessions. Keep the sessions short—no more than five minutes at a time.

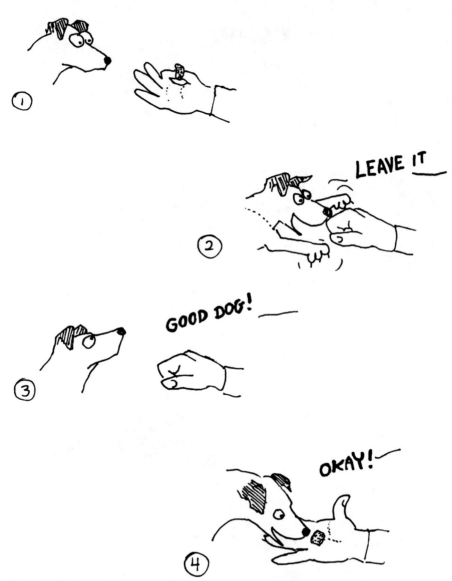

Teaching the Leave It command.

You'll need a good supply of training treats—something not much bigger than one quarter of an inch and preferably dry. We like to sit on a chair for the first two sequences of teaching this command.

STEP 1

Start by holding a treat between your thumb and index finger. With your palm facing up, show the treat to your dog, but don't let him have it. When Felix tries to pry the treat loose say, "Leave it," close your hand around the treat into a fist, and turn your hand so that the back of your hand now faces up. Then observe your dog's reaction. He may stare fixedly at the back of your hand, he may try to get to the treat by nuzzling or nibbling your hand, or he may sit, lie down, or start barking.

Ignore all these behaviors. What you are looking for is the first break in his attention away from your hand. He may make eye contact with you or look away. The *instant* he does, say "Good" and give him the treat.

Repeat several times until your dog looks at you or away from your hand when you give the command "Leave It" and turn your fist over. What you are teaching Felix is that looking at you and not at your hand is rewarded with a treat.

You now have to be careful that Felix is not starting to train you. What is likely to happen is that your dog will look away for an instant and then look right back at your hand, a response you cannot reward. Felix thinks you are trying to train him to *briefly* look away, which is only partially correct. He needs to learn that he has to look away or at you until you say "Good." By not rewarding the incorrect response you can gradually extend the length of time you expect him to look away before you praise and reward.

STEP 2

At this point, you don't know if Felix is responding to the command or the turning of your hand. Since dogs are more sensitive to motion than commands, he likely responded to the turning of your hand rather than the command. To find

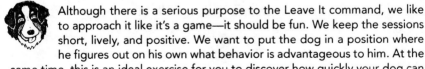

Although there is a serious purpose to the Leave It command, we like to approach it like it's a game—it should be fun. We keep the sessions short, lively, and positive. We want to put the dog in a position where he figures out on his own what behavior is advantageous to him. At the same time, this is an ideal exercise for you to discover how quickly your dog can train you, if you let him.

Hold the leash to prevent the dog from getting the treat on his own.

out, repeat step 1 without turning your hand. If he responds by looking away or at you, then praise and reward. If he does not look away from your hand, then close your hand into a fist and wait for Felix to look away or at you. Repeat until he responds to *only* the command.

STEP 3

The next step is to teach your dog not to pick up something from the floor. Make yourself comfortable sitting on the floor. Show your dog a treat, put it on the floor, and cover it with your hand. When his attention is on your hand or he tries to get to the treat, say "Leave it." Wait for the break in attention and then praise and reward. Now cover the treat with just your index finger. Then place the treat between your index and middle finger. When Felix responds correctly to the Leave It command each time, place the treat one inch in front of your hand. Here you need to be watchful: He may be faster at getting to the treat than you can cover it.

STEP 4

Does Felix now understand the command? Probably, but knowing a command and *reliably* obeying it are not the same. Put Felix on leash and stand next to him on his right. Neatly fold the leash into your left hand, accordion-style, with the

If the dog successfully ignores the treat, praise him and hand it to him.

part that goes to the dog coming out at the bottom of your hand. Hold your hand as close to his collar as is comfortable without any tension on the leash. (The further away the left hand is held from the collar, the less control you have over the dog.) You need to make sure that the slack in the leash does not allow his mouth to reach the floor.

Hold the treat in your right hand and show it to Felix, then casually drop the treat. When he tries to get the treat say, "Leave it." If he responds, praise him, then *pick up* the treat and give it to him. If you let him pick up the treat from the floor, you are defeating the purpose of the exercise.

The Leave It command is not limited to only those objects you don't want Felix to pick up. It is equally useful in situations where you just want Felix to "Leave It"— think of jumping up on the side of a car, lunging at another dog, and similar situations.

If he ignores the command and goes for the treat, pull straight up on the leash and try again. Repeat until he obeys the command. Test his response by taking the leash off and dropping a treat. If he makes a dive for it, don't attempt to beat him to it or yell "no" or whatever. He is just showing you he needs more work on leash.

STEP 5

Now it's time to go outside, but you need to do some preparation first. Select a food item that is readily visible to you in the grass or on the ground, such as some crackers or a few pieces of popcorn. Drop four or five pieces of food in the area where you will take Felix for the big test. Put some of his regular treats in your pocket and take Felix for a walk, *on leash,* in the area where you left the food. Remember to hold the leash short enough so that his head can't reach the ground.

As soon as his nose goes for the food say, "Leave it." If he responds correctly, praise enthusiastically and give him a treat. If he does not obey the command, pull straight up on his leash. If he manages to snag a cracker or kernel of popcorn anyway, you were too slow on the uptake. Since it was your mistake, you can't say or do anything to Felix. Try again, but be a little more alert and prepared to pull up on the leash *before* he has a chance to grab a cracker. His last response to the command has already told you that he will try again. Practice walking around the food-contaminated area until he ignores the food on command.

Felix should now know and obey the Leave It command. Test him off leash and his response will tell you whether or not he needs more work. Still, like any other command, you need to review it with him periodically on leash.

Facts from Felix

1) Teaching the Leave It command is a wonderful opportunity to observe how your dog's mind works.

2) The command is useful to prevent the dog from putting anything in his mouth you don't want him to have.

3) Become aware of how and when your dog is training you.

4) Make this a fun exercise for you and your dog.

5) Don't let your dog pick up treats from the ground.

6) Teach him that you are the dispenser of all that is pleasurable.

Most rescued dogs make wonderful pets.

Chapter 11

The Rescued Dog

Each year, almost four million dogs nationwide wind up in animal shelters and breed-specific rescue organizations; one half never make it out again. The reasons dogs end up in these situations range from the lame—he sheds—to the legitimate—his owner died. Twenty-five percent are purebred, and not the proverbial mutt. The largest percentage of these dogs is abandoned because of so-called "behavior problems," most of which could be avoided by accepting the responsibilities that come with dog ownership—providing a nurturing environment with proper care, housing, and exercise.

Although the majority of rescues make wonderful pets, many come with baggage. Based on our experience, the four most common problems are:

1. Shyness
2. Separation anxiety
3. Overprotectiveness of the new owner
4. Resource guarding

Of course, even a dog purchased as a puppy may develop these problems.

THE SHY DOG

When Helene and her Border Collie, Sparky, arrived at their first obedience class, it was immediately clear to the instructor that Sparky was painfully shy. Sparky came into the room trying to hide behind Helene with his tail between his legs, ears back, and lowered body posture.

For the shy dog, promote confidence rather than rewarding shy behavior.

As the class progressed, it also became clear to the instructor that Helene was feeding into Sparky's shyness. In her misguided effort to help Sparky, Helene would continuously pet him and verbally assure him that everything was all right, and that he had nothing to worry about. What she was actually doing, and quite unintentionally, was rewarding Sparky for his shy behavior.

Cuddle, but don't coddle.

A change in attitude

After the class, the instructor made it a point to talk to Helene about Sparky. Helene told her that Sparky was 8 months old and had been adopted from the local shelter just four weeks ago. She did not know much about his past, but felt that he must have been abused, a common assumption about shelter dogs. Of course, many dogs in a shelter have come from an abusive situation. More frequently, however, shelter dogs are not so much the victims of abuse, but are undersocialized.

Based on her observation of Sparky during the class, the instructor felt that he was shy not because of past trauma or abuse, but because he had not been sufficiently exposed to other people and dogs when he was a youngster (see chapter 1). She advised Helene to take a neutral attitude toward Sparky whenever he showed signs of shyness. Specifically, she was to ignore these signs and under no circumstances try to console him by praising or petting him. Basically, Helene was to follow the "get a life" approach with Sparky. One of our favorite lines from a well-known author and breeder of Yorkshire Terriers is "You can cuddle him, but don't coddle him."

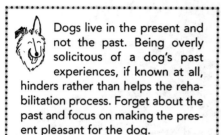

Dogs live in the present and not the past. Being overly solicitous of a dog's past experiences, if known at all, hinders rather than helps the rehabilitation process. Forget about the past and focus on making the present pleasant for the dog.

Helene was to praise Sparky only when he showed signs of confidence, such as holding his ground and not backing up when a stranger approached, and walking down the street with ears and tail erect.

After following the instructor's advice, over the course of several weeks Sparky's demeanor changed. He was more confident in class and in new situations. Of course, participating in the class also helped. At the end of the eight-week program, Sparky behaved just like any other typical Border Collie.

Sitting politely for petting

In addition to making owners aware of how their attitude can increase or decrease a dog's shyness, we like to teach them a specific exercise to build the dog's confidence. The exercise we use is taken from the American Kennel Club's Canine Good Citizen examination. The purpose of this particular test, called "sitting politely for petting," is to demonstrate that the dog will allow the approach of a stranger and permit light petting by the stranger. It is ideally suited to overcome a dog's shyness, and the only prerequisite is that the dog knows the Sit and Stay (see chapter 6). You'll also need a helper.

With your dog Felix sitting at your left side and both of you facing the same direction, begin as you did for the Sit and Stay. Put the leash, neatly folded, into your left hand. The part that goes to the dog should come out under your pinky. Slide the collar around Felix's neck so that the rings are on top and attach the leash. Hold your hand directly above his head, leaving no more than one inch of slack in the leash. Say "Stay." Have your helper—let's call her Mary—stand about

Stranger walks by, no eye contact

Stranger walks by, offers treat, no eye contact

Stranger walks by, briefly pets dog's head, no eye contact

Stranger walks by, pets dog, makes eye contact

Teaching the "sitting politely for petting" exercise.

ten feet in front of and facing you. Tell Mary to casually walk past Felix's left side, keeping a distance of about four feet between herself and Felix, *without* looking at or making eye contact with the dog. When Felix stays, praise him enthusiastically;

if he tries to get up or move away, give him a little tug on the leash, say "Stay," and try again.

When just beginning with this exercise, Felix's response determines how close the helper can get. If after three tries Felix is still apprehensive about Mary's approach, increase the distance at which the helper passes the dog. Find the distance at which Felix holds the Stay and then gradually decrease it to the point where Mary can pass directly by Felix's side. Keep these sessions short—no more than five minutes at a time.

You are ready for the next step when Felix stays without showing any signs of apprehension as the helper goes past. Repeat the previous sequence, except this time the helper offers Felix a treat without making eye contact.

When Felix passes this part of the test, have your helper approach without making eye contact—again in a casual, non-threatening manner—and briefly touch Felix's head as she passes.

Finally, have your helper approach Felix *with* eye contact and then gently touch him on top of the head as she passes. When you have gotten to that point, it is unlikely that Felix will show any signs of apprehension.

The complete sequence looks something like this:

1. Helper/stranger walks by, no eye contact.
2. Helper/stranger walks by, offers treat, no eye contact.
3. Helper/stranger walks by, briefly pets dog's head, no eye contact.
4. Helper/stranger walks by, pets dog, makes eye contact.

The purpose of this exercise is to increase your dog's confidence, so use plenty of patience and praise. The ultimate goal is that your dog, when you tell him to stay, will allow the approach of a stranger and permit the stranger to lightly pet him on the head.

SEPARATION ANXIETY

Separation anxiety (SA) can occur when you leave your dog alone at home—perhaps he is worried of being abandoned again. The most typical and obvious signs of SA are destructive behaviors (chewing or scratching), vocalizations (whining, barking, or howling), house soiling, pacing, and excessive drooling. He is emotionally responding to being physically separated from the person to whom he is attached. Dogs who experience SA are usually high in pack drive and low in defense (fight) drive (see chapter 2), and live in single-dog households. The behavior is rarely seen when there is more than one pet.

In some cases, SA is caused, or at least made worse, by an overly solicitous owner. As the owner prepares to leave the house, he or she makes a big fuss over the dog: "Now don't worry, mommy/daddy will be back soon, but I have to go to work. You be a good boy while I'm gone and I'll bring you a nice treat." Such reassurances only serve to increase the dog's anxiety at the expectation of being left alone. The owner then makes an equally big fuss upon his or her return: "Poor boy. Did you miss me while I was gone? I missed you, too. Were you a good boy?" These utterances actually *increase the dog's excitement in anticipation of the owner's return*. Small wonder the dog becomes anxious!

The "routine" approach

People are just as much creatures of habit as dogs are and tend to follow a specific pattern before leaving the house. This pattern becomes the dog's cue that you are about to depart. Make a list of your customary routine before you leave; for example, putting on makeup, picking up your bag or briefcase, picking up the car keys, putting on your coat, turning off the lights, and reassuring and petting the dog.

To desensitize your dog to this routine, pick a weekend when you don't have to be anywhere specific. At random intervals, several times during the day, go through your routine exactly as you would prior to leaving. Then sit in a chair and read the paper or watch TV, or just putter around the house. By following this procedure, you begin to desensitize the dog to the cues that you are about to leave.

When your dog ignores the cues, leave the house for about five minutes, without paying any attention to the dog. Return without paying any attention to him. Repeat this process, staying out for progressively longer periods. Turning on the radio or TV and providing suitable toys for your dog may also help. Whatever you do, make sure to ignore the dog for five minutes after your return. What you want to accomplish is to take the emotional element out of your comings and goings so your dog will view your arrival and departure as a normal part of a day, with no reason to get excited.

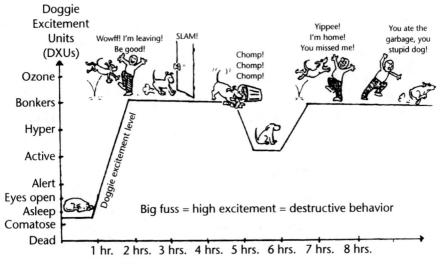

Making separation anxiety worse.

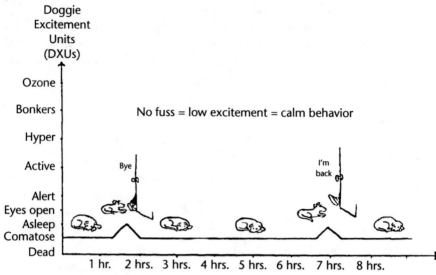

Making separation anxiety better.

The D.A.P. approach

Another way to cope with separation anxiety is to use D.A.P. (Dog Appeasing Pheromone), a product developed by veterinarians that mimics the properties of the natural pheromones of the lactating female. After giving birth, a mother dog generates pheromones that give her puppies a sense of well-being and reassurance.

D.A.P. is marketed in an electrical plug-in diffuser that dispenses the pheromone, which the dog's sense of smell detects. (D.A.P. is odorless to people.) The pheromone reminds the dog of the well-being he felt as a puppy. In clinical trials, D.A.P. was effective in about 75 percent of cases in improving separation-related behaviors. To be effective, the diffuser must be left plugged in 24 hours a day. D.A.P. is available at pet stores and from pet-product catalogs.

OVERPROTECTIVENESS

Having literally been saved by his new owner, the dog may take his duties of protecting him or her a little too seriously. When taken for a walk, he may growl and lunge at strangers when they approach. Perhaps the dog is right, but generally the stranger is harmless and might even be friendly.

Most of the time, the behavior is more of a nuisance than a real threat. The easiest way to deal with it is to make an about-face and go in the opposite direction or cross the street (see chapter 8). If you can't do either, stop, hold your dog on a short leash, and let the stranger pass. Under no circumstances should you reassuringly pet the dog while murmuring, "There, there, it's okay." Felix will perceive that as, "Good dog, keep up the good work," presumably the very opposite of what you want.

When someone comes to the house and is invited in, this overprotective behavior becomes unacceptable. If you don't want to deal with it, put Felix in another room or in his crate. On the other hand, if you want to solve it with training, see chapter 6. Your goal is to have Felix sit quietly while someone is invited into your home. If you are unsuccessful, you may need help from a professional dog trainer.

RESOURCE GUARDING

"Resource guarding" is a term used to describe the behavior of a dog who guards objects of value to him, such as bones, toys, food, or even the couch. Attempts to remove the object, or him from the couch, will be met with growls and possibly biting. In the case of a rescue dog it may be the result of deprivations he has experienced (such as food deprivation). Although the behavior is not unusual, especially for dogs high in prey drive, it is unacceptable and dangerous in a family pet.

Don't inadvertently reward unwanted growling.

Dogs are happy to have a strong pack leader.

We believe in the basic premise that as pack leaders everything belongs to us. The dog is allowed to have only those objects we permit him to have and is required to give up any when asked to do so. For the dog, this is perfectly normal and acceptable pack behavior.

You also need to become aware of your interactions with your dog. Do you give him a treat just because he stands in front of you with a doleful look, or do you first expect him to respond to a command, such as "Sit"? Put another way, is he rewarded just for being cute or for having done something to earn a reward? If you are handing over food to your dog whenever he looks at you, he may interpret this as the submissive behavior of a pack follower and that *he* is actually in charge.

Introducing the Give command

If your dog engages in resource guarding, make sure you have previously established a clear line of communication. Look at the big picture and not a particular behavior in isolation. Review with him exercises like the Sit and Stay—especially when you feed him (see chapter 6)—going through doors (see chapter 6), the Go Lie Down (see chapter 7), and the Leave It (see chapter 10). When Felix clearly understands those commands, he will quickly learn the "Give" command.

What happens when Felix will not give up the object? You need to up the ante.
Maybe your offer to trade was a stale dog biscuit when it needed to be a more tantalizing piece of cheese or chicken. Find the object that will make him trade and you will succeed.

The Give command is an extension of "Leave It" and is used when the dog already has something in his mouth that you want him to put in the palm of your hand. "Drop It" is used when you just want him to spit it out. The teaching process is the same. The commands differentiate only between whether you want the dead fish placed into your hand or dropped to the ground where it may rest in peace.

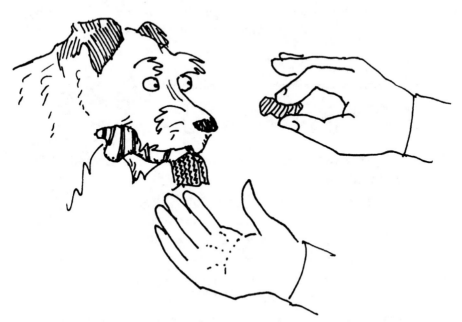

Teaching the Give command.

Teaching the Give command

You need to know what your dog's favorite treats are because teaching the Give command involves a trade: Felix has something in his mouth that you want. When you are teaching the command, start with trading a treat for one of his toys. To get Felix to give up the toy, you offer him something that he would prefer. The key word here is *prefer*. Usually, that something is a one-half-inch cube of food, such as a piece of steak, fish, cheese, etc. (if he has just snagged the steak you were going to prepare for dinner, you are in trouble). Say "Give," offer him the tidbit with your left hand, and hold your right hand, palm up, under his chin. When he puts the object into your hand, verbally praise with "Good dog," and give him the treat. The verbal praise is important and must be sincere—the ultimate object being to use treats *randomly* and rely mainly on praise. (Remember to change the command to "Drop It" when you want him to spit the object on the ground.)

As Felix catches on, begin to minimize the treat, then only randomly reward with a treat, but verbally and warmly praise him every time he gives up his object. After you have gotten to the point where he looks at you expectantly as you approach, begin calling him to you and ask him to give up the object. Since you now have changed the rules, the first few times you call him to you, reward him with a treat.

From then on, verbally praise for every correct response and randomly reward correct responses with a treat. If resource guarding continues to be a problem, even after your training efforts, it's time to consult a professional dog trainer.

Facts from Felix

1) A rescue dog can make a wonderful companion.

2) Dogs live in the present and not the past.

3) For the shy dog, teach Sitting Politely for Petting.

4) Use the "routine" approach to stop separation anxiety.

5) Resource guarding is another training opportunity.

6) Learn to trade with the Give command.

7) Do not reassure the dog when he is growling at strangers. The dog will misinterpret this as being praised.

Chapter 12

Objectionable Behavior

I f you have followed our advice in the previous chapters, you may never need to read this one! If you skipped the first part of this book and turned immediately to this chapter, go back and start at the beginning. Most dogs respond well to basic training, and many objectionable behaviors can be resolved by establishing a line of communication with your dog, which is the main purpose of training.

YOUR OPTIONS

In the event some unacceptable behavior persists, you have four options:

1. Tolerate it.
2. Train.
3. Find a new home for your dog.
4. Give up.

Tolerate it

At first blush, this may not seem like much of an option. Then you begin to consider the amount of time and energy that would be involved in dealing with your dog's annoying antics and you may decide that you can live with them after all. You tolerate the way the dog is because you are not prepared to put in the required effort to train him.

Tolerate

Train

Find new home

Give up

Four options for dealing with objectionable behavior.

Train!

You have decided that you cannot live with such a dog and that you are going to train him to be the pet you expected and always wanted. You understand this will require an initial investment of time and effort, perhaps even expert help. But you are willing to work to achieve your goal—a long-lasting, mutually rewarding relationship. Good for you!

For most people, dog ownership is a compromise between *toleration* and *training*. Jack's Standard Wirehaired Dachshund, Cece, is housebroken and crate trained, comes when called (mostly), and stays when told. However, all this training has not shaken Cece's conviction that her purpose on this Earth is to practice her landscaping skills, which she does with enthusiasm and determination. Jack, in turn, has learned to tolerate her efforts.

> After all is said and done, the best route for you is to take an active part in training your dog. There is no substitute for creating that special relationship with your dog than through spending time with him to train him. If you want your dog to look up to you as his "hero," then train him!

Find a new home for your dog

Your dog's temperament may be unsuitable to your lifestyle. A shy dog or a dog with physical limitations may never develop into a great playmate for active children. A dog who does not like to be left alone too long is not suitable for someone who is away from home all day. While most behaviors can be modified with training, others cannot, or the effort required to do so would make the dog neurotic.

In some instances the dog and the owner are mismatched and need to divorce. The dog may need a great deal more exercise than the owner is able to give, and as a result the dog is developing behavior problems. Whatever the reason, under some circumstances placement in a new home where the dog's needs can be met is in the best interest of both the dog and owner.

Give up

If all else has failed and you find you just can't live with this dog, the remaining option is to deliver him to a shelter. It is not something to be taken lightly and should be considered only when you have really tried to work it out and there are simply no other alternatives. Although animal shelters work hard to place dogs and other animals, due to the large volume of unwanted and stray animals in this country he faces a 50 percent chance of being euthanized. A no-kill shelter may be an option if you are lucky enough to live near one, but there is often a long waiting list because of their no-kill policy.

If you have a purebred dog, your best option may be a breed-specific rescue organization. Such groups are usually not shelters in the traditional sense, but they go to great lengths to save a dog of the breed they love. Breed-specific rescue organizations can be found on the Internet or local kennel clubs may have information about them.

If your dog is truly dangerous toward people and cannot be rehabilitated, it is unethical to try to pass him off to an unsuspecting stranger. Euthanasia may be the only option that is left. Consult your veterinarian for guidance.

WHY DOES YOUR DOG DO IT?

Many owners believe their dogs misbehave out of spite. They are indignant at what they perceive to be the dog's lack of gratitude. After all, "I house you, I feed you, I take care of all your veterinary expenses, the least you can do is not chew up my shoes!" Unfortunately, dogs are not grateful and don't know what the word means.

The objectionable activity—barking, chewing, digging, or whatever—is rewarding in and of itself. Your dog does not lie awake at night thinking of ways to aggravate you, but acts to satisfy a need. For example, barking, chewing, and digging are associated with boredom and tension. The dog engages in the particular behavior because the activity relieves the boredom or tension. It can also be attention-getting behavior. For a dog who wants attention, almost anything, even being scolded, is better than no attention at all.

The easiest way to stop a behavior is by dealing with the need that brought it about in the first place, rather than trying to correct the behavior itself. Punitive approaches cause your dog to be afraid of you and undermine the very relationship you are trying to build. Moreover, as we've mentioned, punishment after the fact is pointless since the dog does not associate it with his "bad" behavior.

So-called behavior problems are often the effect of some cause and not a cause in and of itself. Find the cause and you can cure the problem. Lack of sufficient exercise, isolation and mental stagnation, health and nutrition problems, and unintentional training are the main causes for a variety of objectionable behaviors.

Lack of sufficient exercise

The most common reason for objectionable behavior is lack of sufficient exercise. A Labrador Retriever is a hunting dog with a high energy level. Cooped up in a house all day, the dog may take to shredding the couch to get rid of that energy. Determining what is a sufficient amount of exercise for your dog depends on his age, size, breed, and energy level, but it is usually much more than you think.

Isolation and mental stagnation

Your dog does not need you to be his full-time entertainment center, but extended periods of being left alone may make your pet a neurotic. Problems associated with isolation are excessive barking, chewing, digging, and sometimes self-mutilation.

Dogs don't lie awake nights thinking up mischief. There is always a reason for problem behavior!

The unfortunate result of lack of sufficient exercise.

For pack animals like dogs, isolation results in mental stagnation.

Dogs are pack animals and need interaction with the "pack" members—that is, you and your family. Just being together is often enough, but training is even better. Doing something for you on a regular basis makes your dog feel useful and provides the mental stimulation he needs.

Physical or health problems

The leading causes for a *sudden* change in behavior are physical or health problems. A normally obedient dog suddenly refusing to sit, for example, may have developed arthritis, a spinal disorder, or infected or impacted anal glands.

Physical problems are often the cause of aggression and biting. If biting is a problem, you *must* do something about it because it is only a matter of time before you face legal difficulties.

A recent study shows that a lengthy list of behavior problems, including aggression, can be attributed to hypothyroidism, which is an underactive thyroid. This condition affects almost 50 percent of the entire dog population. Fortunately, it is easily treated with inexpensive medication, but it *must* be treated. When you notice a sudden behavior change, such as a lack of interest in activities that he normally enjoys, your first course of action should be to take your dog to your veterinarian for a thorough checkup. Request a blood test that includes a *complete* thyroid panel. Even if the results show that his thyroid is functioning in the low end of the normal range, the dog may benefit from medication.

Health problems can be a source of objectionable behavior.

Improper diet

Diet can be responsible for a variety of behavior problems, including hyperactivity, difficulty in housetraining, and slow learning. Not all dogs can tolerate corn, soy, wheat, etc., or beef, chicken, or lamb. You also need to consult your veterinarian to find out whether your dog has allergies to substances contained in his

Read the labels to see what your dog is eating!

food. Allergies can range from chemical additives and food coloring to one or more of the main ingredients in the food. Your dog may also have nutritional deficiencies that require special supplementation.

It's wise to be an informed consumer, so read the label on the dog food bag or can. Two of the first three ingredients listed on the label should be animal protein sources such as chicken or beef, not just by-products. Your vet can recommend some high-quality dog foods.

Unintentional training

Biting behavior can be triggered by roughhousing with your dog, teasing by children, mistreatment, tension or violence in the household, or fear.

Roughhousing is a particularly problematic form of "play." Brandy started out as a sweet puppy. The children delighted in playing with her and she never caused any difficulties. Dad even took her to obedience class, where she graduated at the top of her class.

Several months later, problems developed. While being taken for a walk by Mom, Brandy started a tug-of-war with the leash. When Mom tried to get her to stop, Brandy growled. She also became too rough for the children, who did not want to play with her anymore.

Roughhousing can result in unintentional training.

When Dad called us with this sad tale asking for advice, it did not take too long to learn that he liked to roughhouse with Brandy. He saw nothing wrong with it since he was able to keep Brandy under control when things got too rough. We explained to him that he had taught Brandy to become rougher and rougher, but that Mom and the children could not control her. He was to stop all the rough play and review the obedience exercises.

Fortunately for Brandy, the story has a happy ending. Once Dad quit the fooling around and spent more constructive time with her, Brandy became her sweet old self again.

In a nutshell, good behavior requires the following:

- Good exercise
- Good company
- Good health
- Good nutrition
- Good training

Good company, exercise, health, nutrition, and training are all part of good behavior.

WHAT TO DO ABOUT UNACCEPTABLE BEHAVIOR

If you find a particular behavior unacceptable, look for its cause and deal with it accordingly. Once you have ruled out the physical or dietary aspect, tackle the problem with exercise and training—spend more time with your dog. If the problem persists despite your best efforts, consult an expert.

In-house help

In-house help is an option, if you don't mind paying the price—it tends to be expensive. It works something like this: A consultant or trainer comes to your house, talks to you about your dog, and then recommends a course of action that is expected to solve the problem.

In-house training is an option.

Theoretically, it is the ideal solution to an owner's problem with the dog because the consultant or trainer can see firsthand what the dog is doing and make the appropriate recommendations.

If you are interested in the services of an in-house consultant or trainer, ask your veterinarian to refer you to such an individual. As with all trainers, be sure to check the individual's training credentials *thoroughly* and ask for references.

Boarding your dog to be trained

Another option, which is also expensive, is to send your dog to a boarding facility that specializes in training. Three weeks is the customary minimum.

Training tends to focus on general obedience, which may or may not address your particular problem. For example, if Felix soils or shreds your drapes, that behavior needs to be dealt with in the environment where the drapes are.

Boarding your dog to be trained can be useful.

Since your dog will stay at this facility, you have to be especially careful in its selection. Where will your dog be housed? What will be the daily schedule? How often will he be exercised? When and what will he be fed? What methods will be used in training?

Finding the right place may not be easy. Whatever you do, inspect the facility and observe some of the training before you leave your dog, and ask for references. Your veterinarian or a local boarding kennel may be able to recommend a facility.

Going to school with your dog

A good option is to enroll in an obedience class. Although classes tend to be geared to teaching traditional obedience commands, such as Heel, Come, and Stay, most obedience instructors are able to advise you on a wide range of topics.

We are in favor of classes because they are economical and get *you* involved in the training process. Your dog also learns to behave around other dogs—a big advantage.

Before you commit yourself to a class, attend one or two sessions and watch. Following are a few pointers to help you select a class:

- Is the atmosphere friendly?
- Do the dogs seem to enjoy the training?
- Is the instructor pleasant and courteous to the human students in the class?
- Does the instructor appear knowledgeable?
- Do you like the way the dogs are being treated?

Going to class with your dog trains both of you!

- Would you want to treat *your* dog that way?
- Do the dogs visibly progress in the training?

If you are not satisfied with what you see, visit another class. There are usually more than one and sometimes quite a few dog-obedience groups that train in any given area. Not all use the same approach to training; if you don't like the way one operates, try another. You are looking for a club or a school that trains in accordance with your own personal values. Presumably you have your dog because you like him—so train that way! Consult your yellow pages and look for an obedience club or training school in your area.

Doggie day care

Over the past ten years there has been an explosion of doggie day-care facilities. For many dog owners the availability of doggie day care is a godsend. Busy lifestyles often leave little time for the family pooch and fitting "together time" into the schedule is hard. For most of his day, the dog is pretty much left to his own devices. And when you return in the evening from a hard day at work and perhaps an even harder commute, there is little energy left for Felix who is now raring to go.

Enter the doggie day-care facility. You can drop off Felix before going to work and pick him up again on the way home. During the day, Felix spends much of his time playing with other dogs, taking an afternoon nap, and playing some more. Many facilities also offer training. Whatever the situation, Felix comes home after a hard day of horsing around with his canine pals feeling just as tired as you. Tired dogs have happy owners!

Doggie day care works well for those on a tight schedule.

I WILL NOT CHEW THE RUG.
I WILL NOT CHEW THE RUG.
I WILL NOT CHEW THE RUG.
I WILL NOT CH

Facts from Felix

1)   In dealing with your dog's behavior you have a variety of options, the most important one being training.

2)   Dogs do not behave badly out of spite.

3)   To stop behavior, address the need that brought it on in the first place.

4)   Lack of sufficient exercise is the most common reason for objectionable behavior.

5)   Good behavior requires good exercise, good company, good health, good nutrition, and good training.

6)   If you don't have the time or inclination to train your dog yourself, have someone do it for you.

Epilogue

Using the approach to training described in this book, we have found that most dogs are quite content to go along with the program. More than that, they enjoy it and look forward to their regular training sessions.

If you believe your dog will not love you anymore when you train him, you are in for a surprise. Quite the opposite is the case; training will make your dog *more* affectionate toward you. Through training comes respect, and through respect comes love.

With training, you give your pet a job that makes him feel needed and wanted, which is important for mental well-being. You also give your dog some exercise, which is important for physical well-being.

When you experience what you perceive as a problem, ask yourself, "What is *my* responsibility toward its solution?" We start with the basic premise that it is rarely the dog's fault. If you truly do the same, the solution will come to you. On the other hand, if you always blame your dog, your relationship is doomed to fail.

Dogs demonstrate daily that they are our best friends. Now it's your turn to demonstrate that you deserve that friend.

Bibliography

Bergman, Goran. *Why Does Your Dog Do That?* New York: Howell Book House, 1971.

Campbell, William E. *Behavior Problems in Dogs.* Wenatchee, WA: Dogwise Publishing, 1999.

Evans, Job Michael. *The Evans Guide for Civilized City Canines.* New York: Howell Book House, 1988.

Lorenz, Konrad. *Man Meets Dog.* New York: Penguin Books, 1964.

Most, Konrad. *Training Dogs: A Manual.* Wenatchee, WA: Dogwise Publishing, 2000.

Pfaffenberger, Clarence J. *The New Knowledge of Dog Behavior.* New York: Howell Book House, 1963.

Pryor, Karen. *Don't Shoot the Dog!* New York: Simon & Schuster, 1984.

Volhard, Jack, and Gail T. Fisher. *Training Your Dog: The Step-by-Step Manual.* New York: Howell Book House, 1983.

_____. *Teaching Dog Obedience Classes: The Manual for Instructors.* New York: Howell Book House, 1986.

Volhard, Jack, and Wendy Volhard. *Open and Utility Training: The Motivational Method.* New York: Howell Book House, 1992.

_____. *The Canine Good Citizen: Every Dog Can Be One.* New York: Howell Book House, 1997.

_____. *The Complete Idiot's Guide to a Well-Trained Dog.* Indianapolis: Alpha Books, 1999.

_____. *Dog Training For Dummies.* Indianapolis: Wiley Publishing, 2005.

Volhard, Wendy, and Kerry Brown, DVM. *Holistic Guide for a Healthy Dog.* New York: Howell Book House, 2000.

Index

CPSIA information can be obtained at www.ICGtesting.com
Printed in the USA
LVOW09*1409130616

492389LV00004B/19/P